THE HOLY GRAIL

THE HOLY GRAIL

LEGEND OF THE WESTERN WORLD

FRANJO TERHART

Bath · New York · Singapore · Hong Kong · Cologne · Delhi · Melbourne

CONTENT

This is a Parragon Publishing Book

Copyright © Parragon Books Ltd
Queen Street House
4 Queen Street
Bath BA1 1 HE, UK

Original edition: ditter.projektagentur Gmbh
Project coordination and picture research:
  Irina Ditter-Hilkens
Editing: Sabine Baumgartner
Design and layout: Claudio Martinez

American edition produced by APE Int'l
Translation: Dr. Pippin Michelli

ISBN: 978-1-4054-8972-0

Printed in United Arab Emirates

The Grail in Literature and Music 18

The Christian Grail Tradition 48

Important Grail Traditions in Europe 70

Galahad, son of Lancelot, was the noblest and purest knight of all. Of all the dedicated Grail-seeking knights of King Arthur's legendary round table, he was the only one who actually found it.

THE HOLY GRAIL

A Western legend

The Holy Grail, with its multiple, dense layers of legend, continues to present mysteries today, and is probably the best-known myth of the West. What is so magical about this belief in an enigmatic and symbolic object with magical effects? What exactly is the Grail? The questions remain unanswered. Indeed, even its name has not yet been clarified. Is it a cup, a bowl, a jewel from Lucifer's crown, a meteorite, a container for

the blood of Christ, a pseudonym for the Shroud of Turin, or the heretical symbol for the idea that the blood of the Crucified in the Grail cup refers to his physical descendants, as Dan Brown suggests in his runaway bestseller *The Da Vinci Code*? These questions have gone unanswered for close to a thousand years. Yet many have aspired to solve the riddle of the Grail, including the Cathars, the Knights Templar, the Freemasons and the National Socialists of the Third Reich. It has also been the theme of countless Hollywood films.

The linguistic origin of the Grail

Even the Grail's origin as a word is disputed. It may derive from the Old French *gradalis*, a deepened container in which food was served sequentially in small portions. These were a common item at many medieval courts. But it would be too humdrum to reduce the Grail to a mundane household effect—and in any case the Grail legend embraces a variety of traditions, that have led, over time, to a blend of Celtic, Christian, and Oriental legends and ideas. One of these claims that the cup was used at the Last Supper, before Jesus was condemned and crucified. The wealthy merchant Joseph of Arimathea was a

Is the Grail the cup of the Last Supper that Jesus used before his death? Is it a bowl or container in which Joseph of Arimathea caught some of the blood pouring off Jesus at the cross? Or is it a symbol for the physical descendants of the Savior?

friend of Jesus. Standing under the cross, he caught some of the blood of the Savior in a cup, possibly the above-mentioned cup of the Last Supper. Later he traveled to Glastonbury in southern England and buried the Grail there at the spring known as the Chalice Well.

The literary sources

In the original and incomplete *Perceval* text written by Chrétien de Troyes, dating from the year 1180, it is nowhere explicitly stated that the Grail is a cup or bowl. Rather, it is said to resemble a stone (or, more precisely, a meteorite). The same is also true of Wolfram von Eschenbach's account. In Sir Thomas Malory's novel, *Le Mort d'Arthur*, which developed in the mid-fifteenth century, as well as in many other texts from the thirteenth century, the Grail is described as a golden container that contains some of the holy blood of Jesus Christ—the very one that Joseph of Arimathea entrusted to future generations. The power of the Grail is described as overwhelming. Its incandescent light is intolerable to the impure, which may be a way of intimating that the Grail can only be perceived by its seekers after an extensive period of initiation. Historically, it seems that the concept of the Grail is closely associated with the myth of good and evil: the light fights against the darkness, the soul against its captivity in the material body. The Grail can be won only by those who are pure, without sin, and with lance and sword in hand.

An old story

Just how old the legend of the Holy Grail is, cannot be clearly established. The Grail itself is difficult to comprehend and has retained all of its legendary mystery. This publication introduces all the twelfth- and thirteenth-century literary sources for the Grail that were reworked by Richard Wagner for his opera *Parsifal*, written in 1882. Grail seekers such as the Templars and Cathars are described in some detail, as well as possible locations of the Grail in France, Spain, Italy, and England. Various Grail concepts are also examined in depth, including the theory that Jesus and Mary Magdalen had children and that the Grail is somehow a testament to this.

THE ORIGINS OF
THE GRAIL LEGEND

A MYSTERIOUS BRETON HERMIT

The monk's chronicle

One reference to the possibility that the Grail saga is even older than the literary sources that have been passed down to us is given at one point in the chronicle of a certain monk named Helinandus of Froidmont. As the author Franz Baumer explains, the monk wrote, "at that time (717–719), an angel gave a Breton hermit a marvelous vision of a face, that of the the noble decurion Joseph who took the body of Christ down from the cross, and of the dish with which the Lord shared a meal with his disciples. The hermit wrote a description of that vision, a history that is known as the *Gradale (Of the Grail)*. The *gradalis* or *gradale* was the name of a slightly deepened dish in which sumptuous meals were served in stages to the wealthy at court in the Frankish empire.

The individual servings were arranged in graduated rows ... it was popularly called the *graalz*."

The hermit's Grail

The name of the Breton hermit who experienced this vision is certainly well-known: it is Waleran. This hermit apparently had a vision of Jesus on the cross and of a dish of the kind used at that time in many noble houses. This would have been a wide dish in which meals were served in successive courses, and the word *gradale* refers to these courses. In the better houses, such utensils were called *graalz* in the vernacular. Thus the question arises whether this term really refers to the *Grail*. In this respect, it is telling that Chrétien de Troyes also uses the term Grail in a way that assumes all his readers would know what he

Traces of the Grail in Brittany
Near the forest of Brocéliande (where the magician Merlin's grave lies, according to legend), stands the chapel of Tréhorenteuc. At the behest of the local Catholic priest, artists created three unusual church windows here between the years 1942 and 1962. The central window shows the Grail lit up by flames. It glows at the center in the form of a turquoise-colored cup. Two angels unfurl a banner bearing the text, "the cup of my blood." Christ and Joseph of Arimathea are shown among them. The other two windows show the Grail at the Last Supper and appearing at King Arthur's round table. It is green at the Last Supper and turquoise at the round table; the latter denotes the Holy Spirit, while at the Last Supper green is a reference to the emerald that Lucifer lost from his crown when he fell to earth.

The little chapel of Tréhorenteuc in Brittany was furnished with scenes from the Grail cycle. Thus the windows of this church show the knights of the round table, along with King Arthur and the Holy Grail.

meant by it. The poor hermit claims that the blood of Jesus was caught in a deepened plate such as this. For him, therefore, the communion bowl is identical to a *graalz* of this kind.

According to the Gospels, at the Last Supper Jesus held up a cup of wine and explained to the twelve disciples that the wine had become his blood. Could this be the origin of the Grail mystery?

The authenticity issue

The monk who recorded Waleran's tale, Helinandus of Froidmont, explains that he found only one copy of the hermit's text with its vision, and it was written in the French language. Furthermore, the text was incomplete, and in fact the owner did not want to let him see it directly, so Helinandus could not determine its age at all. The nobles who were in possession of the hermit's text prevented any investigation of the manuscript, which supposedly dated from the eighth century. Thus, the existence of this Breton hermit cannot be established. But the hermit's text also alludes to Nicodemus, who had a conversation with Jesus by night after his crucifixion, as Robert de Boron later wrote in his own text, *The Romance of the Saint Graal*. As a result of this commonality, some scholars believe that the hermit's text was written after Robert de Boron's book of ca. 1200, and that it cannot date from the eighth century.

The hermit Waleran, who may have been in Brittany as early as the eighth century, is said to have been the first to mention the Holy Grail. Unfortunately, this source cannot be satisfactorily verified.

The Celts called the world beyond this one the Otherworld, while in the legend of Arthur it is called Avalon. By either name, the Celtic Otherworld is always hidden from the living by a dense mist.

CELTIC LEGEND

Celtic cultural concepts

There is a significant core of Celtic material in the Christianized Grail legend. Chrétien de Troyes, whose narrative will be discussed in greater detail later (see pp. 20ff.), was a Frenchman, not a Celt. Nonetheless, research has shown that for his Grail narrative, he relied on Celtic traditions that probably existed only in oral form at that time (eleventh century). It is generally accepted that the origin of all the Grail legends that emerged after Chrétien de Troyes is to be found in the Irish *echtrae* (adventure). This typically Irish form of legend describes the Celtic world beyond this one (Otherworld, as they called it) as a paradisical island. Various heroes—such as Cormac, a legendary Irish king who arrived in the Otherworld one day with the help of an enchanted branch—experience the world of the dead there, where day never ends and life is indescribably pleasant.

Celtic adventure journeys

The *echtrae* (plural: *echtrai*) is a narrative of the fantastic voyage by which a human hero comes to the island realms and the palaces of the gods and immortals. There, the living men are regaled with exquisite meals served in golden dishes that are never empty. Food and drink are always available in abundance. No one ages, becomes ill or dies there. Magical swords and supernatural spears endow their owners with powers that do not exist in the material world. *Echtrai* readers learn of the "cauldron of rebirth," the self-replenishing cornucopia, and other cauldrons that bestow wisdom and immortality. All this appears in modified form in the later Grail legends, albeit enriched with Christian motives and ideals and monastic archetypes.

The wounded king

A further motive found in Grail legends was adopted from the ancient Celtic stories. In the Grail castle languishes a king: the Fisher King. He has a mysterious wound in his thigh, and therefore cannot govern his country. Some scholars conclude from this that the king is impotent, and that as a logical consequence his country has become a barren desert.
Both the Celtic *echtrai* and the Grail narratives contain this motive. In the Celtic understanding, a wounded king was unable to govern his country, as there was a direct relationship between the general well-being of the country and its people and the wholeness of their king. This is a further remarkable parallel between the Grail narratives and the Celtic *echtrai*.

The Celtic rule of succession

All of the various Grail legends also describe a form of the rule of succession. The ill and ageing king seeks to confer his rule onto a younger man who has been chosen or designated. The young man has no suspicion of this, however, and will only gain the crown if he addresses the correct questions to the sick king. The Grail plays a significant part in this motive, as it is a magical object that does not originate from this world. In the Celtic *echtrai*, as well, rulership is transferred from one generation to the next through a magic object after the hero has passed a test of this kind. For example, in the story of **The Phantom's Frenzy**, there is a magic cup or grail with an important function similar to that in the Grail narrative. Like the Christian Percival, the Celtic hero Conn must ask a question, "Who is served with this cup?" Only then can he become the successor of the dying king. The Christian authors borrowed this motive, as well, from the Celtic *echtrai* in their Grail narratives.

The Grail narratives are always concerned with the rule of succession. Only if the hero asks the sick and dying king the correct question, can he inherit crown and kingdom.

The Celtic cult of the head

Another Celtic motive that is found in the Grail romances is the beheading scene. Often when knights join in battle against each other, the outcome is only decided when one opponent succeeds in killing the other by beheading him. This frequent motive in the Grail texts indicates their closeness to Celtic thought, in which a marked cult of the head is characteristic. The head contains thought, and therefore also all supernatural qualities, since thinking was understood as divine intuition. The Celts believed that separating a head from its body through the use of manly skill and strength would capture its life essence. The more heads a man won in battle, the more powerful he became, and the his status rose proportionally. There is one further snippet of interest in this connection: turning a severed head 180 degrees forms a container, or a cauldron, while the head continues to serve as a sort of container for the supernatural. Thus, metaphorically, an inverted head may also represent the Grail and/or an identical container.

The richly decorated Gundestrup cauldron is a treasure trove of imagery and information for Celtic scholars. The detail shown above illustrates a fallen warrior being placed into the cauldron of life, in order to emerge from it alive, but unable to speak.

The Dagda

For the Celts, there were even gods with several heads and/or faces. One of these is the Dagda, who possessed a magic cauldron. The Dagda was admired as a triune god and lord of life and death. He continually renews and maintains the cosmos (on a similar principle to the Holy Grail) and feeds all who follow him. He uses his cauldron—which carries the eloquent name *Never Dry*—for this purpose, and everyone who is entitled receives food from it. The Dagda is the arch magician, the god of the Druids, the priest of the Celts, and his companions are the elves. Thirty-two images of the Dagda, the triune Celtic god, have been found so far. Of these, the face on the vase from Bouvay (kept in the Bibliothèque Nationale, Paris), shown below, is considered a very fine example.

The Celtic cauldron

A cauldron is a huge cooking pot. It became a many-layered symbol in Celtic mythology, and in some cases they were made of very costly materials. Archaeological and textual sources confirm that this kind of pot was an utterly sacred ritual container for the Celts. Many Celtic gods used the cauldron as a cult object to form a sort of bridge between this life and the Otherworld. In the *Mabinogion*, a Welsh collection of legends that was first written down at the end of the eleventh century, it is narrated that the Ghael (i. e., the Old Irish) lit a fire under a cauldron that was believed to be a "cauldron of resurrection." They filled this cauldron

The Celts believed that by cutting off the head, they received the life essence of the slain person. This cult of the head found its way into the Grail narratives.

with the corpses of their fallen warriors, who awoke back to life the following morning. Although they rose to fight again, they could not speak, as it is not fitting for any living person to find out too much about life in the next world, or Otherworld. The *echtrai*, which include descriptions of the realm of the dead, were thought to provide enough information for a living person's needs.

The Celtic Peredur, precursor of Percival

With regard to his name, the Welsh hero Peredur (a Celt) is seen as a precursor of Percival. The Peredur legend has it that a horse with a corpse in its saddle cantered up to him one day. A woman immediately came and took the body from the horse, washed it in a cauldron, and then anointed the body with precious unguent. A little while later the man awoke to new life, and made "a cheerful face." These uniquely Celtic conceptions of the strength and power of the cauldron as a giver of life are found again in the Grail legend. They are clear excerpts from the Celtic cultural ethos that found their way into Christendom through the Christianization of old paganism in Western Europe.

Might the Grail legend have originated not in Europe, but in Palestine? Some scholars believe so, supporting their thesis on Wolfram von Eschenbach's version of the Grail tradition.

EASTERN CONNECTIONS

Oriental elements

The majority of Grail scholars believe that the Grail legend has its origins primarily in the Celtic area, i.e., in and around Western Europe. Several factors support this assumption, including the miraculous cauldron of the Dagda that provides an infinite abundance of food and raises the dead, as well as the magic spear of the Celtic god of light, Loucetios, and the functional similarity between the Celtic *dysgl* bowl and the Grail.

The cloth and the stone, and their Arabic archetypes

As corroborative evidence of their belief that the Grail legend has Arab origins, the "orientalists" point to Wolfram's concept of the Grail as a stone, which the poet connected with the stars. By this, Wolfram meant the Black Stone in the external wall of the Kaaba in Mecca—a meteorite. Both the Muslims and Wolfram believed it came to Earth by means of angels. The green cloth on which the Grail is borne, and also its name (the Cloth of Achmardi), stem from the Arabic. However, the strongest proof he cited in support of his thesis was the inscription that appears on the Grail. It is written in Arabic, and it means "The Radiant One."

But there are convincing arguments in favor of seeing the source of the Grail concept in another part of the world entirely: the Orient. Some Grail narratives mention a city that is the basis of the contention that the Grail is of non-European origin. That city is Sarras (or Saraz), and the proponents of this thesis support their assertions mainly through Wolfram von Eschenbach's version of the Grail legend, his epic poem "Parzival." Sarras may be understood as a synonym for the Saracens (Muslims) or as the city of Sahr-Azzah in Palestine. In Wolfram von Eschenbach's lifetime (ca. 1170–ca. 1220 or 1230), the Saracens were in control of much of Spain. Finally, in the interest of completeness, it should be mentioned here that Sarras is also the name of a city in the Valley of Ardèche in southern France.

The root of Percival's name is Arabic. The great composer Richard Wagner (1813–1883) gave the name Parsifal to the Grail seeker in his opera of the same name, as it derives from the Persian word for "pure fool." This assumption was later supported by the scholar Frederick von Suhtscheck (1883–1944), who investigated the apparently close conceptual relationships between the names in the Grail cycle and ancient Persian ideas. According to Suhtscheck, an old Persian text, "The Story of the Pearl," mentions a castle called Mount Schalwadea, in which he saw a strong resemblance to Wolfram von Eschenbach's Montsalvat (or Montsalvaesche). In Persian, Parsi means pure in the same religious sense as the Cathars ("the pure ones") used it. To become the Keeper of the Grail, Percival had to be pure of all worldly desires, sinless, and devoted to God—an idea that probably originates from a Persian or Islamic worldview. Further support for this theory is provided by Percival's father (Gahmuret), who fought for the caliph of Baghdad, according to Wolfram's account. This is nothing short of astonishing, since it suggests that a Christian knight had placed himself in the service of the Muslims. However, all these hypotheses lack clear proof. Despite their plausibility, therefore, they remain mere supposition.

The holy Black Stone of the Muslims (possibly a meteorite) is set into the exterior wall of the Kaaba in Mecca. Could this be the origin of Wolfram von Eschenbach's concept of the Grail?

The Grail legend: a variety of sources

There was clearly no single original history on which all the Grail authors depended. Chrétien de Troyes was one of the first to bring the various motives together into a Grail cycle. In the twelfth and thirteenth centuries, a conflation of different sources occurred in the Grail synthesis. Irish *echtrai*, Welsh ballads, Islamic esotericism and mysticism, Persian influences and astrological ideas, as well as pagan and Christian concepts of the mother goddess all flow together in the Grail legend.

THE GRAIL
IN LITERATURE
AND MUSIC

CHRÉTIEN DE TROYES: PERCEVAL, OR LE CONTE DU GRAAL

A textual source?

Chrétien de Troyes is a primary source for the Holy Grail, as he was the first to turn this cycle into a literary topos. Thus, like some heavenly guiding star, he led the way for the many authors who came after him. In the current state of research, some scholars of the Middle Ages argue that Chrétien de Troyes invented the Grail outright, that it was to all intents and purposes his own idea. However, the fact remains that

Chrétien claimed to have a documentary source on the existence of the Grail. Although it has not yet been possible to substantiate this, it also cannot be disproved. Some scholars consider a direct descendant of the House of Alsace, Dietrich of Flanders, to be that source. In 1150, on his return from the Second Crusade, he brought back from Jerusalem a reliquary

The various Grail stories developed in the West as the crusaders were finally losing their supremacy in the Holy Land. The deeds of the Grail seekers were first told in the European courts.

containing a few drops of blood caught by Joseph of Arimathea at the crucifixion. It is likely that Chrétien de Troyes intended to refer to the connection between this reliquary and the Grail at the end of *Perceval*. It was never added, however, as he died before he was able to complete the work. Nonetheless, Robert de Boron made this motive a feature of his own *Roman de l'Estoire dou Graal* some ten years later.

Chrétien de Troyes' *Perceval*

An inexperienced youth undergoes a test without realizing it. The objects in this test are a spear and a dish. The test consists in his finding someone who can give him information about the spear and dish, and can explain who is served by them. In the final analysis, this concerns discovering the meaning of the two mysterious objects. The person who can give him the information is an invalid who could be healed by answering this question. Perceval finds the invalid, but fails to ask him the crucial question and thus dooms him to further suffering. When he discovers the consequences to the sick man, he tries to make good his failure and ultimately succeeds in doing so. He then becomes the guardian of the two treasures (the spear and dish), while his predecessor is healed. This, very briefly, is the plot of Chrétien de Troyes' *Perceval*

The Grail narratives always concern a young man, such as Perceval, who leaves his castle, wife, and children to look for the Grail, a mission that involves many trials and tribulations. He travels by boat to strange lands no one has ever seen.

(which Chrétien also called *Le Conte du Graal*). The actual history of that mysterious object, the Grail, remains obscure. The French author is only interested in the destiny of young Perceval, and pays less attention to the spear and the dish on which it relies.

Perceval's Grail

The story told by Chrétien de Troyes in his most famous work is that of an inexperienced youth who matures into the ideal knight. In his inexperience, he makes many mistakes due to the fact that, in certain situations, his behavior runs counter to human and social expectations. Thus, he fails to ask the ailing Fisher King, in whose castle he sees the spear and the dish (that is, the lance and Grail), about these two objects. Although they are shown to him several times, he refrains from asking because he had been told previously that a good knight does not talk too much or express curiosity. But in this particular situation, he should have asked the correct question, because the Fisher King was seeking a successor—who could only be Perceval.

Galahad fights the "seven knights of darkness." This engagement symbolizes the dangerous quest for the Holy Grail, which can also be won through the use of the sword and the lance.

The lance and the graal

The Fisher King lives in the City of the Grail with his servants and invites Perceval to an evening meal there. Before the meal, a squire enters the hall bearing a lance from whose point fall gouts of blood. After this squire comes a second bearing candles, and a noblewoman with a "graal." The author does not use this word as a name, but as the established term for a wide dish of gold, as was commonplace at that time. This *graal*, or grail, is carried past Perceval several times without his asking who is served by it. Each time the grail appears, it produces food and drink in plenty, because it is the function of a *graal* to be a choice serving dish. As the reader discovers later, the grail contains a Host (Communion wafer), a reference to the body of Jesus Christ in the Catholic Mass. What the hero Perceval does wrong is not explained by the author.

The Swiss Gate is the entrance to the oldest wing of the Imperial Palace, which is also where the treasury is.

Seeking the secret of the Grail

The following morning Perceval leaves the castle of the Fisher King with no further encounters. No one bids him farewell, thus he seems to have done something wrong without knowing it. Only in the thick of the forest does he meet a maiden who weeps for her dead friend, who has been decapitated. She blames Perceval for his behavior to the Fisher King. Later, at King Arthur's court, he swears that he will not rest until he has discovered the secrets of the bleeding lance and the Grail. For five long years he seeks the castle of the Fisher King, defeating sixty outstanding knights and undergoing several adventures. In all the years of his search, he never entered a church, as he had completely forgotten God. A hermit he meets asks Perceval to confess his sins and godlessness, and then explains to him how he failed in the City of the Grail.

The Grail seeker becomes the ideal knight

Chrétien de Troyes does not tell us how the story of Perceval continues. The romance remained incomplete and was only brought to a conclusion by Wolfram von Eschenbach, who has Perceval become the Fisher King's successor. He wins this succession because, in the Christian understanding of the time, he has fought successfully against sin in the world and in himself. Perceval's appointment to the Grail is a spiritual turning point, as previously described by Bernard

of Clairvaux in his treatise *In Praise of the New Knighthood*, by which he meant the Knights Templar.

Everything that Perceval experiences leads towards his finding himself, and thus ultimately to his encounter with God. In the teaching of St. Bernard, his is an individual path towards the realization of God that bypasses the rituals of the Church. At its heart, this process applies to Perceval. Through his unswerving search for the Grail, he matures into the ideal knight, and ultimately is recompensed with the rulership of the Grail King.

British sources report that Helena was born and raised in Colchester. Her husband Constantine was proclaimed emperor in York. Prior to her marriage, she was known as Princess Elaine, the Greco-Latin form of Helen.

WOLFRAM VON ESCHENBACH: PARZIVAL

A *Thyngge* called the Grail

According to Wolfram von Eschenbach, the heathen Flegetanis solemnly declared that he truly had read in the stars of a *dinc* (*thyngge*, or thing) called the Grail. This perfect *thyngge*, added Flegetanis, was preserved by a line of Christians dedicated to the pure life. The appointed Keeper of the Grail would become the greatest of all people. All the Grail Kings belong to a family, of which Parzival is also a member. While the Grail is tended by virgins, it is protected by knights of the Grail.

It goes without saying that the knights themselves never revealed their true names, and if the origin of the Order of the Knights Templar is sought in the twelfth and thirteenth centuries, this is because Wolfram von Eschenbach called them *templeis* in his work. The German author was reluctant to credit Chrétien de Troyes as the source for his *Parzival* material, claiming rather that it was communicated to him by a mysterious person called Kyot. Kyot, in his turn, claimed to have discovered an ancient,

This illumination shows Wolfram von Eschenbach in the guise of a knight with his squire, preparing for a tournament. Wolfram was the only medieval author who called the guardians of the Grail *templeis* (Templars).

hitherto ignored Arabic text on the Grail in Toledo, Spain. Wolfram provided no details about this text, and scholars tend to doubt whether Kyot referred to it at all.

Who was Wolfram von Eschenbach?

Wolfram von Eschenbach was born ca. 1170/75 in the Frankish town of Eschenbach quite close to Ansbach. Hardly anything is known about his life (similar to Chrétien de Troyes), except that he seems to have earned his living as a troubadour. Nor is it known who commissioned him to write the 24,810 verses of *Parzival*, but he probably was familiar with Chrétien de Troyes' *Perceval*. It can be shown, however, that he was related to Count von Wertheim and some aristocratic families in Styria. His main patron is thought to have been Hermann of Thuringia, after whose death in 1217 Wolfram's literary output seems to have been silenced. Finally, Wolfram's death has not been established, but he is believed to have died in Eschenbach sometime after 1220.

If Wolfram von Eschenbach had spent any time in Toledo, he surely would have been aware of the ancient church of San Juan de Reyes. This is where some claim that he was initiated into the secret of the Grail by Kyot.

Who was Flegetanis?

Parzival contains a great deal of astronomical knowledge for the time in which it was written, and the pagan figure of Flegetanis is a symbol for this. He is depicted an educated Jew, knowledgeable about Judaeo-Chaldean astronomy, who converted to Christianity. "To the circling course of the stars man's affairs and destiny are linked. Flegetanis," Wolfram explained, "could tell us how all the stars set and rise again and how long each one revolves before it reaches its starting point once more." But who was this Flegetanis, really? All the evidence suggests that he was not a historical figure, but rather the transliteration of an ancient Arabic book, whose title *Felek Thani*, roughly translated, means the "second celestial sphere." Thus Flegetanis represents the astronomical and astrological knowledge of his time. The reference to the Grail in the stars creates its cosmic significance. Furthermore, Wolfram's references to Flegetanis include an eternal bloodline and predictions of future events.

The Grail: a stone from the stars?

The plot of *Parzival* generally runs along the same lines as the plot of Chrétien's book. Parzival, too, is welcomed into the castle of the Fisher King (who is named Amfortas), and is served by the Grail. But the Grail is no longer a dish: it is a *thyngge* with its own history. It is now a stone named *lapis exillis*, or "stone of the stars," that fell from heaven (thus, some kind of meteorite) and reposes on an emerald-green silk cloth. Only a pure virgin, the Grail Bearer, can lift it because of its "dreadful" weight.

Even today, the Templars are an enigmatic order. It is a fact that they were wealthy and powerful, and among other things, were collectors of legendary treasures. They are thought to have been in possession of the Ark of the Covenant and the Grail.

The British actor Nigel Terry played the role of King Arthur in the 1981 film *Excalibur*. In it, King Arthur is portrayed as the archetypal strong, just king who champions the true faith and fights on behalf of his people.

Who was Parzival?

An important part of the legend of the Grail as it has been passed down to us is Parzival, Perceval, Peredur, Perlesvaux, Parsifal or "Son of the Widow," as Chrétien de Troyes also calls him. It is he who undertakes the difficult quest for the Grail and regains it only after defeating many courageous knights in battle. Who was this Perceval or Parzival? It is discovered that he was the aristocratic and legal successor of the Fisher King. Academics took an early interest in the interpretation of his name. In translation, the name Perceval means "pierce-the-vale" (or, metaphorically, "deep-in-the-heart," or "right-through-the-middle"). Wolfram von Eschenbach, especially, had a tendency to treat the interpretation of a character's name as part of their personality. Someone named Perceval or Parzival is a man whose name indicates fighting prowess and determination in pursuit of a single goal.

The pure fool

Richard Wagner made yet another interpretation of the name in his opera *Parsifal*. The move from Parzival to Parsifal was quite deliberate because he liked the derivation from the Arabic word *Parseh-Fal*. This word means "pure fool" or "poor idiot," and this is indeed the character of Wagner's Parsifal at the outset of his Grail quest. Over time, however—and this is made very clear in Wagner's opera—the "pure fool" develops into a mature, intuitively wise, and empathetic person. This kind of development had already been initiated by Chrétien de Troyes, whose Grail King took many years to evolve from an inexperienced knight. In addition to courtly and knightly behavior, he learned to fight evil, both in the world and within himself, since only the noblest knight could find the Grail and become its guardian.

Parzival's early education

In his youth, Parzival was a fool. As Wolfram von Eschenbach has it, this was primarily because his mother, Herzeloyde, wanted to prevent him from becoming a knight. But after he met four knights during his childhood, that was young Parzival's sole desire. Seeing only their dazzling armor, he seriously

This illumination, dated 1286, shows Perceval with the Grail. Only through this vessel can the wilderness inherited from the ailing king be made fertile again.

Parzival: a hero for today?

To a far greater extent than in the earlier Grail legend, Wolfram's Parzival is a hero on a quest for the truth of the utmost urgency. This is a deeply lonely road to follow. In the Middle Ages, and even more so today, this theme spoke to readers, as it spotlights the position of the individual within society as a whole. For medieval people, everything was ordered according to the will of the Church. Wolfram's Parzival, however, was a very human skeptic on a search for God and the truth.

The ruins of Tintagel (the legendary birthplace of King Arthur) were discovered on the coast of Cornwall. Better still, astonishingly, archaeological excavations unearthed a clay shard bearing Arthur's name.

believed them to be angels. From the four knights, Parzival heard about King Arthur for the first time and decided to become a knight himself. When his mother realized that she could hardly prevent him, she dressed her son in peasant garb and furnished him with an old nag for a horse. After his departure, Herzeloyde died of grief. Meanwhile, Parzival set out like a complete lunatic. Gauche and erratic, he solved his problems in simply absurd ways. Before he could become a great knight, he first had to mature. Undertaking the Grail quest thus initiated a process of development that had to be experienced within himself, in his life, and in the world in order to achieve purity. Wolfram von Eschenbach makes this completely clear as his hero goes through three stages. Firstly, he slowly awakens from his neglected, lumbering unconscious state; then he experiences suffering and doubt about everything and everyone; and finally he achieves illumination.

Wolfram's concept of the lance

Wolfram von Eschenbach puts great value on certain things, and carefully reconstructed familial relationships are especially relevant in this respect. Two families emerge: the family of the Grail (the Titurels) and the family of Arthur. Through his father, Parzival is connected to the aristocratic French house of Anjou, and through his mother he is related to the Grail King Amfortas. The lance (which for Chrétien was yet another reference to the lance of Longinus) is completely re-interpreted by Wolfram. Wolfram's lance also drips with blood, but this is the blood of the Grail King, rather than Jesus. For Wolfram, the lance serves as a kind of medical instrument, as it helps the king draw blood from his poisoned body. Amfortas was wounded in the testicle by a poisoned lance. When the poison settles there as ice, it must be removed with the lance and a silver knife.

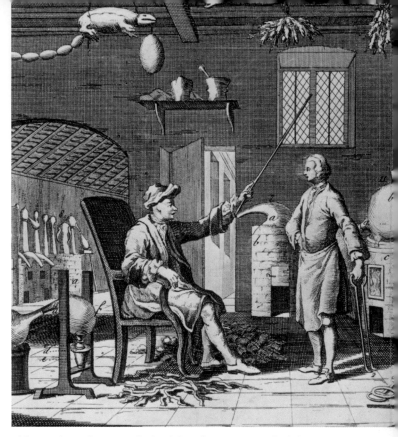

Alchemists have always sought the philosopher's stone. Grail scholars have a theory that the Grail is synonymous with the philosopher's stone. This is partly based on Wolfram von Eschenbach's reference to the mysterious *lapis exillis*.

The Grail as philosophers' stone

The Grail stone receives its power anew every Good Friday in the form of a dazzling white dove that places the Host (Communion wafer) on it, which makes it possible for the Grail to provide all foods in super-

The fresco of the Grail Bearer Repanse de Schoye in the chapel of Tahull in the Spanish Pyrenées.

The chapel of Tahull

Hidden in the high mountains of the Catalan Pyrenées, the early Romanesque chapel of St. Climente has stood on the Tahull plateau since the twelfth century. In it one can view what is probably the earliest of all medieval representations of the Grail. The Virgin Mary—or, better, Repanse de Schoye—with wide open eyes gazing into the distance, raises a dish in her left hand from which multiple rays of light emanate. The Grail Bearer's face is unusually long and seems a little odd. The Grail dish is presented on a blue-green cloth that falls in long folds as part of her magnificent cloak, recalling von Eschenbach's cloth of emerald-green silk. The Grail is found in the hands of a divine virgin, a motif that alludes to life-giving abundance. This is an archaic idea that has been associated with mother goddesses throughout the ages.

abundance. At the same time, the Grail bestows immortality upon those who look on it. It may be asked whether the *lapis exillis* is comparable to the stone of destiny (which is the alchemists' philosopher's stone, used to purify matter and raise people to physical and spiritual perfection). Another possibility suggests that the stone is comparable with the one that lies in the Kaaba at Mecca. This black stone is almost certainly a meteorite that fell from heaven, which would make the *lapis exillis* more accurately *lapis ex caelis*. According to alchemical lore, healing forces are bound to stone, and this may be one reason why the Grail King's bed was decorated with forty-four noble stones or gems.

Peyrepertuse in the Pyrenées was a Cathar stronghold. As with the Knights Templar, it was rumored that they had the Grail in their possession. For that reason alone, the Church would have pursued them inexorably.

The virgin Grail Bearer

Scholarly research has demonstrated that there are close ties between the Grail legend and the cult of the Virgin. But this connection only emerged over the course of time. For Wolfram von Eschenbach, the Grail rested in the hands of the virgin Grail Queen Repanse de Schoye, whose name means something like "giver of joy." In von Eschenbach's *Parzival*, Repanse de Schoye marries Parzival's dark-skinned, heathen brother Feirefiz, who is later converted to Christianity. Their son is Prester John, who was mentioned for the first time in the chronicle of Otto von Freising (died 1158). His legendary kingdom was later assumed to be Ethiopia, but for Wolfram's continuator he became Parzival's successor as Grail King.

Old Glastonbury lay in the middle of a marshy floodplain and became known as the Isle of Glais. Glastonbury Tor crowns a hill that rises out of the plain like an island, and is a magical point of attraction for all tourists.

ROBERT DE BORON: LE ROMAN DE L'ESTOIRE DOU GRAAL

A trilogy with a mysterious origin

Between 1191 and 1202, Robert de Boron wrote a trilogy under the title *Le Roman de l'Estoire dou Graal*, which contained three books in verse form: *Joseph d'Arimathie*, *Merlin*, and *Perceval*. These relate, among other things, how the Grail cup came to Britain. Other

topics covered by the trilogy include the rise of King Arthur, the round table, the search for the Holy Grail, and the decline of King Arthur's golden age. Robert de Boron states at the beginning of his book that he cannot betray its source because writing about the Grail is a great secret. In a later elaboration, de Boron claimed this great book was in fact written by Christ himself, and that he received it from the author in an English abbey. De Boron's trilogy connects the mysterious sacred vessel of the Grail directly with the Holy Eucharist, something no author before him had done. In addition, he identifies the one who caught the blood of Jesus in a chalice: Joseph of Arimathea, the wealthy merchant in whose own tomb the crucified Jesus was buried.

Who was Robert de Boron?

It is believed that Robert de Boron was a cleric and in the service of Count Gauthier de Mont-béliard, who died at the beginning of the Fourth Crusade, launched in 1204. Only a single manuscript of De Boron's *Roman de l'Estoire dou Graal* (*Romance of the Story of the Graal*) has survived. Its style, in contrast to that of Chrétien de Troyes, is unrefined and straightforward. It is not clear if his work was written before or after Chrétien's, though de Boron claims unequivocally to be the first to record the history of the Grail. Some scholars argue that he spent time in England at the court of Henry II. If so, he would likely have been acquainted with the Celtic-Christian legendary tradition surrounding Glastonbury Abbey.

Arthur, Glastonbury, and the Celtic cauldron

Chrétien de Troyes had already connected the Grail narrative with the world of King Arthur. Robert de Boron expands the story by having Joseph of Arimathea travel from Palestine to Avaron (Avalon) in southern England with the Grail cup. Avalon is identified as Glastonbury, site of the important medieval abbey that saw itself as "the Jerusalem of the West." In 1190, the monks of that abbey claimed to have discovered the bodies of King Arthur and his wife Guinevere (see pp. 34ff., 86). Glastonbury was the starting point for the Christianization of the Celtic world and the site of England's first chapel dedicated to Mary (the Lady Chapel, the former *vetusa ecclesias*), which King Arthur may even have visited. Even before that, Glastonbury was a place of special significance for the Druids.

The lonely knight on horseback riding through the country fighting against wrongdoers was a common motive among nineteenth-century Romantic artists, including Ferdinand Leeke in his 1912 painting, *Parsifal in Quest of the Holy Grail.*

The Celtic Grail

For the Celts of the British Isles, all of Glastonbury functioned as a cosmic image of the cauldron—the miraculous bowl or tureen so crucial to the Celts—that was thought to rest in the depths of the earth. This magical cult vessel from the distant past had life-giving properties. It was a sacred symbol for the Celtic religion, and it is also the pagan root of the Christian Grail. Robert de Boron may have been familiar with this ancient Celtic tradition and incorporated it into the sacred symbolism of his own Christianity.

It should also be remembered that the Celtic cauldron was filled with blood. In Robert de Boron's trilogy, Joseph of Arimathea brings the only true Grail—the chalice containing the blood of Jesus—to Glastonbury. In a strange way, Glastonbury Abbey and Celtic mysteries melded with the worldview of early Christianity. The wealthy merchant from Jerusalem and the Holy Grail thus formed the Christian version of the pagan legend and in the process became a powerful instrument of evangelism.

Contrasts between Chrétien de Troyes and Robert de Boron

If one compares de Troyes' and de Boron's books on the Grail, the tremendous differences in the views of the two authors are brought to light. Robert de Boron describes the present and shows its historic development. His purpose is to explain the origins of the Grail and what happened in relation to it later. Chrétien de Troyes, on the other hand, describes the future development of the Grail. He presupposes his audience's familiarity with the history of the Grail, and does not explain its existence further. Some scholars insist vehemently that de Troyes' adopted de Boron's term *Graal*, although it cannot be clearly established whether that is really the case. Regarding the Grail itself, Chrétien emphasizes the Communion wafer as the converted body of Christ. De Boron has the blood of Christ collected in the vessel and its efficacy is derived through its purely spiritual power. Both poets include a scene in which secret words are spoken. In de Boron, only the Grail bearer Bron hears these; in de Troyes, Perceval is the one who hears the words spoken by the hermit on Good Friday. It may be asked why either poet drew attention to these secret formulae at all. Interpretations range from affiliations with secret societies to references to ancient mystery cults. The secret words can also be taken to indicate that there were strict requirements of silence with regard to the secrets of the Grail.

Robert de Boron's Grail etymology

If Robert de Boron really was the originator of the term Holy Grail, as some medieval scholars believe (although this is a matter of debate), then the etymological origin of the word may be easily inferred. The first time the word *graal* occurs in de Boron's epic is when Joseph of Arimathea sets up a table in memory of the Last Supper. When he asks the group gathered with him what the symbolic vessel should be called, the answer is '*Graal* (Grail)'! "For no one sees the Grail, I believe, who does not find it agreeable. It pleases everyone in the land, it is agreeable and good to all; it fills those who see it with delight if they can bear to be near it." It is in this new capacity as a

The fish as a symbol of Christianity
For both de Boron and de Troyes, the fish (as found in the wall paintings on Roman catacombs of the earliest Christian communities) has an important function as a symbol of Christ. Christ appeared on earth as the Son of God during the Age of Pisces. Both poets connect the Christ-fish with the Fisher King, seeing them as symbolic of humankind's desire for Christ's salvation.

Communion chalice that the Grail becomes identified as the 'Holy' Grail.

The poet strains the etymology of the word *graal* when he derives it from the French *agréer* (to please). In de Boron's understanding, the Grail is something that "pleases everyone," as can be seen in the above excerpt. Whether that speech is an accurate attribution may be doubted, however, as Robert de Boron states elsewhere that he had heard *l'Estoire dou Graal* and only later set it down in writing. Thus it is possible that his interpretation of the origin of the word *graal* is based on his own assumptions, rather than on fact.

The Grail takes many forms, including a chalice, a dish, and a cauldron. It is most often presented as a chalice such as the one used by Jesus at the Last Supper. The more magical it looks, the more genuine it must be!

Bron and the Celtic Bran

There is an odd similarity between the names of Bron the Grail Bearer and Bran, the Celtic god who possesses the Cauldron of Plenty. With it, Bran could raise the dead back to life. In one fight, Bran was mortally wounded in the foot with a poisoned spear (recalling the motive of the Fisher King in the Grail saga) and asked his friends to decapitate him and bury his head in the White Tower of London. Thereafter, the head had the ability to foretell the future and kept Bran's followers supplied with all necessities—such as food.

Who exactly was Joseph of Arimathea? Scholars say that there has never been a place named Arimathea, and the Bible offers no explanation of the nature of the connection between Joseph and the family of Jesus.

GEOFFREY OF MONMOUTH, CREATOR OF THE ARTHUR LEGEND

Who was Geoffrey of Monmouth?

Little is known about the life of Geoffrey of Monmouth, either. He is known to have been born ca. 1100 and to have lived in Oxford between 1129 and 1151, probably working as a tutor. Between 1149 and 1151 he wrote the *Vita Merlini* (*Life of Merlin*), shortly after his successful *Historia Regum Britanniae* (*History of the Kings of England*). Later he was appointed bishop of St. Asaph in Wales, although he never took office due to political unrest in the country. He died in 1154. His first book, *Prophetiae Merlini* (*The Prophecies of Merlin*), written ca. 1135, received as much attention in his own time as the prophecies of Nostradamus later did during the Renaissance.

First reference to King Arthur

Geoffrey of Monmouth is the first surviving source to mention Arthur, in his *Historia Regum Britanniae*. His history of this heroic British king spread throughout the whole of Christendom remarkably quickly. By the time of the Crusades, everyone was familiar with Geoffrey's work and thus also with Arthur's twelve legendary battles against the barbarian ideas of the Angles, Saxons, and Picts. In the figure of Arthur, the poet seems to have given the twelfth century a symbol of hope. Arthur became the glorious king and chosen one, the ideal knight, the epitome of loyalty and noble courage. The best knights in the world came together at his castle, Camelot.

As early as 1165, King Arthur was already represented in an extensive floor mosaic in the cathedral of the southern Italian city of Otranto. In the arch over the north portal of the cathedral in the northern Italian city of Modena, a complete scene from the life of King Arthur is carved in stone. As this relief was completed between 1110 and 1130, the artist must have conceived the idea even before Geoffrey of Monmouth's publication reached Italy.

It is now established that King Arthur (or Artus) was a real person. In his *Vita Sancti Columbae* (*Life of St. Columba*), Abbot Adamnan reported that King Arthur, son of Aedàn, fell in the Battle of Camlann.

Arthur, a genuine historical figure

The relief at Modena cathedral, above which is chiseled the inscription *Arthur de Bretania*, shows that various stories that have circulated about this king, then and now, are apparently based on fact. Owing to a strong culture of oral history, ancient Celtic stories were long remembered by the people. Geoffrey of Monmouth put them in written form, probably for the first time, in his *Historia Regum Britanniae*. The author even explains to readers that Arthur was the son of Uther Pendragon and nephew of Aurelius Ambrosius. Aurelius Ambrosius is documented in the fifth century by the retreating Saxons as a British army leader with a Roman name who fought against them in 410 CE.

Heathen raids and the promise of the Grail

In the same year, the Goths, led by King Alaric, conquered Rome and robbed the city of the treasures of the Temple of Jerusalem (such as the famous seven-armed candelabrae), which had been carried off by Emperor Titus in the year 70.

Probably also at that time, the cup of the Last Supper was secretly brought to San Juan de la Peña Monastery in the Pyrenées (see pp. 74ff.). This period, not long after Christianity had been declared the state religion by Emperor Theodosius I in 381 CE, was a highly symbolic and eventful one for Christianity. As a result of pagan attacks (by Goths and Saxons), the country returned to chaos. In this context, a charismatic ruler like Arthur might well have seemed to act as God's chosen agent.

Christ himself remained among men as the assurance of salvation in the blood of the Grail: this was the Grail's promise. It is surely no coincidence that Helinandus should have mentioned the Grail as early as ca. 717, after the country had endured a period of apparently unceasing battles and upheaval.

Merlin the wizard (here pictured with his lover Viviane) is also thought to be based on a real historical figure, a Druid. Thus we can identify a Druid named Myrddin, who lived and worked as a seer and poet during the sixth century.

Arthur: name or title?

Painstaking research has led two English authors, Graham Phillips and Martin Keatmann, to argue that the historical Arthur was actually named Owain Ddantgwyn and bore the title *Artus*. Owain Ddantgwyn was the son of one of the kings of Gwynedd (Wales) who was dubbed High Dragon—which is the meaning of the Celtic name *Pendragon*. In his time, ca. 500 CE, Owain Ddantgwyn was the most powerful ruler in Britain and father of Cuneglaus—whose forbear was known as "Bear," which is *Arth* in Welsh, the first syllable of "Arthur." Bear is therefore almost certainly the origin of the name *Arturus*. This name was conferred on the strongest army leader as an honorary title. Owain Ddantgwyn fell in the Battle of Camlann in 519, the very place where Geoffrey of Monmouth sets Arthur's death. With him died the last ruler of a united Britain which had emerged from the Roman Empire. At that time the spiritual and religious roots of the country (Celtic and Christian) were threatened by invaders, and with Arthur's death a nostalgic nationalistic mythology rapidly formed around the last great king of Britain.

Riothamus and Arthur

King Arthur is frequently equated with a fifth century CE British king named Riothamus, who led his army to subdue unruly British colonists overseas on behalf of the Romans. However, historians have discovered that Riothamus, too, is not a name but a title. Derived from the original British form *Rigotamos*, it means something like *Over King* or *High King*. The *Rigotamos* was a designated ruler who had jurisdiction over a combined kingdom. Since the titles *Artus* and *Rigotamus* appear to be synonymous, it may be argued that Owain Dtantgwin was High King of Britain and thus seen as guarantor of its peace.

In the Middle Ages, people revered megalithic graves as the burial places of important figures. One example is "Merlin's Grave" in Brittany, and another (seen here) is "King Arthur's Grave" in Newport, Wales.

The Arthurian knights' search for the Holy Grail

King Arthur's famous round table, at which only the finest knights in the land found a place, had been created for a single purpose only. According to Geoffrey of Monmouth, this was to spread the truth of the Grail everywhere. The Knights of the Round Table therefore also became known as the Knights of the Grail. But only one of these, Lancelot, would be worthy of serving the Grail. After a long and arduous search in which he almost despaired, Lancelot finally arrived at a castle guarded by two lions. Hearing singing behind a door, he knew that he had found the resting place of the Holy Grail. Somewhat later, he would see the holy vessel covered with a cloth of red and gold silk brocade in a radiantly bright chamber. He also saw an aged priest surrounded by angels and holding up a Communion wafer. Three men wanted to place an object in the priest's hands, but it seemed much too heavy for the priest. When Lancelot sought to help him, this happened: he felt he had been shot through with fire and was rooted to the floor, unable to move. He was unconscious for twenty-four days. On coming to, he found himself at Castle Corbenic.

Frederick Hamilton Jackson painted *Lancelot's Vision of the Holy Grail* in 1893. Accompanied by angelic spirits, the knight rises upwards, as do all enraptured earth dwellers. In this way, the Grail may be seen as a heavenly breakthrough into the world.

Corbenic, the eternal horn of plenty

Behind the strange name of the castle lurks a reference to the Holy Grail. *Corbin* or *Corbenic* is the cornucopia that is never exhausted. It provides an endless bounty of food, both physical and spiritual. *Cor benic* means "blessed horn." *Corbenic* may also refer to the Celtic word *corben* (raven). Castle Corbenic, which probably belonged to King Bran Fendigaid (Bran the Blessed, see p. 33), is located in Wales. According to a Welsh legend, this king had been wounded by a spear (like the Fisher King) and sought a magical cauldron that could bring about rebirth. The myths and legends that rose around Castle Corbenic offer yet another example of the Grail's strong Celtic connections.

Corbenic is the cornucopia that never fails. Its rich bounty corresponds to an old belief held by the Celts in Britain that nature is eternal. It is never depleted, but is constantly renewed.

GRAIL ROMANCES AFTER 1215

The Vulgate Grail Cycle

In addition to the four best-known literary sources (Chrétien de Troyes, Wolfram von Eschenbach, Robert de Boron, and Geoffrey of Monmouth), there are other manuscripts that take up the Grail, most of them produced within years of those first publications. One of these is the very extensive prose collection known as the Vulgate Grail Cycle, which was apparently developed between 1215 and 1235 and was probably written by several authors. The collection comprises five works, including *l'Estoire del Saint Graal* (History of the Holy Grail), *l'Estoire de Merlin* (Life of Merlin), the *Lancelot Propre* (Prose Lancelot), the *Queste del Saint Graal* (Quest for the Holy Grail), and *Le Mort de Roi Artu* (The Death of King Arthur). The authors may have produced the works for the Cistercians, as monastic ideas—such as the search for God, celibacy, monastic community, and so forth—play a central role in the texts. At the same time, the narratives also include countless references that betray knowledge of the Apocryphal Gospels, as well as texts that the Church had rejected as heretical.

Lancelot, Galahad, and Gawain

The Vulgate Cycle is so named because it was written in the vulgar tongue, that is the language of ordinary people. In this version of the legend, names other than Percival emerge in connection with the Grail quest. The selection of Lancelot is long and quite complex. In fact, the young man was baptized with the name of Galahad, but later became known as Lancelot. Even more confusing is the fact that Lancelot's son is also called Galahad, and he was the purest and truest Grail-seeking knight in the world. Lancelot's foster mother was a fairy who only reluctantly let her son follow his

Lancelot with his lover, Queen Guinevere, wife of King Arthur. This sinful liaison was another important aspect of the legend of King Arthur.

The *siege perilous*
The *siege perilous* (literally, "dangerous seat") at King Arthur's famous round table is a seat that is always kept vacant. Only a true and perfect knight could take his place there without grave risk—hence its name, *siege perilous*. When the young Galahad arrived at the court of King Arthur, he inadvertently sat on that particular seat—and nothing happened. Galahad was also the only one, other than Arthur, who could pull the magic sword Excalibur out of the stone.

The Lady Guinevere

The beautiful and seductive Queen Guinevere, wife of King Arthur.

The best knight in the world

At a tournament at King Arthur's court, Galahad won the white shield on which Joseph of Arimathea once painted a red cross with his own blood. Galahad proved himself the best knight in the world when he defeated both Percival and Lancelot, neither of whom knew who their opponent was. Like Galahad, though, both Lancelot and Percival would have experience the reality of the Grail. Lancelot had his vision of the Grail alone; in the Vulgate Cycle, Percival and another knight join Galahad at the City of the Grail. In *Queste del Saint Graal* we read that at the end of their quest, they arrived at Corbenic, City of the Grail, where they were joined by Galahad and nine more Knights of the Grail. It is no coincidence that this group of twelve recalls the twelve apostles. After the twelve knights had gathered, Joseph

The nineteenth-century American artist Edwin Austin Abbey used an angel to represent the idea of the Grail as a heavenly thing in his painting *The Infant Galahad—First Sight of The Grail*. Angels symbolize the domain of the holy.

calling. Lancelot was also the sinful knight who desired and won the favor of Arthur's queen, Guinevere. After many triumphs in many adventures, Lancelot succeeded in entering the City of the Grail, where he was able to break the curse on a maiden who had been imprisoned in a cauldron of boiling water. As a result of this rescue, the Grail King recognized Lancelot as the appointed father of the true Grail knight. Only Lancelot's son, Galahad, would be able to bring the Grail quest to a successful conclusion. The maiden Lancelot had freed from the curse became Galahad's mother. She tricked Lancelot into impregnating her by using an enchanted drink that made him think he was sleeping with Queen Guinevere.

of Arimathea descended from heaven and they all celebrated the liturgy of the Grail, in which the knights witnessed the transformation of the bread into the body of the Lord Jesus Christ. Joseph explained that the Grail is the Communion chalice, and the knights then witnessed the crucified Jesus rising from the Grail.

Sir Gawain

Unlike Percival, Gawain (or Gauvain) was a lay knight who hungered for adventure. His task included retrieving the sword with which John the Baptist was beheaded. He did so after killing an evil king and wresting that very sword from him. He returned it to the Grail King. When he saw the bleeding lance and the Grail he became enraptured, and each time he saw the Grail he

Countless artists have discovered the King Arthur material and filmed it for cinema or television. The new, alternative King Arthur was made in Ireland in 2003 by Antoine Fuqua. This scene shows the Round Table Knights Galahad (left) and Gawain (right).

Perlesvaus, a tale of magic and power

Written at the beginning of the thirteenth century (1205), *Perlesvaus* is the third great Grail epic written in Old French. The unknown author was familiar with the works by Chrétien de Troyes and Robert de Boron, since he makes direct references to them. *Perlesvaus* is an intense combination of magic and violence, religion and esoterica, which mark the author as a free-thinking spirit with anarchic tendencies. Decapitated heads appear several times in the novel, including those of Adam and Eve, which shows that the work was informed by Celtic beliefs such as the cult of the head. A motive found in no other Grail romance is that the Grail can change its form, changing from a bowl to a chalice. Its main feature is the restoration of youth.

received another vision. Thus he saw a small child, three drops of blood, candles, and the Crucified Lord. But he was silent about all he saw, and was therefore no longer allowed to enter the chapel in Grail City.

The Post-Vulgate Cycle

The unknown author of this epic focuses entirely on the history of the Grail, also including the adventures of a few noble knights and the death of King Arthur. In this cycle, the Grail is a divine instrument that will heal the country of all ills if it can be found. The book was likely written ca. 1240 CE, probably by someone within the Cistercian order.

The most important Cistercian of the time was Bernard of Clairvaux, whose works included the rule for the Order of the Knights Templar. The Templars, of course, were believed to be keepers of the Grail, another testimony to the fact that the idea of the Grail was spread throughout Europe by like-minded people. Bernard of Clairvaux is known to have esteemed Celtic religious ideas. A deep Christian faith in the power of the Holy Blood, mixed with the striving for perfect knighthood and a strong Celtic tradition are all reflected in the Grail literature of this period.

BERNARD
The Life of Bernard, who dyed An. Chrifti 115

No one knows whether Bernard of Clairvaux was interested in the Grail, but it may be significant that he wrote the rule for the Order of the Knights Templar and submitted it to the pope in 1129 at the Council of Troyes.

THE GRAIL THROUGH THE LENS OF THE LITERARY SOURCES

The origin and derivation of *Grail* as a word

The origin of the very word *Grail* is ill-defined, thus leaving plenty of room for speculation. Just as the thing it signifies is understood by some to be a stone and by others a Communion chalice, by some to be the blood of Christ and by others as the bloodline of the Savior, or in yet another variation, some identify it with the shroud of Turin and others with the *volto santo* (Veronica's veil), the meaning and origin of the word *Grail* cannot, in fact, be established. The term therefore remains mysterious—which was probably precisely the intention of the various authors.

Etymological explanations of the word *Grail*

Listed below are some of the most commonly cited explanations for the word *Grail*:

Is the Grail nothing more than a meteorite, a stone fallen from heaven that fascinated medieval people purely because of its inexplicable origin? Wolfram von Eschenbach seems to have believed so.

Many Grail narratives mention a Communion wafer in addition to the chalice or dish. This represents the body of Jesus, which was given for all humankind through his sacrifice on the cross.

- *Grail* derives from the Latin *gradalis* or *gradatim*, which means gradual or gradually, and refers to a dish in which meals are offered in a certain order.
- *Grail* comes from the French *agréable*, which means pleasant or pleasing.
- *Grail* is derived from the German *graolen*, which means to celebrate in a noisy or rowdy way.
- *Grail* comes from the middle high-German noun *Graol*, which means a miraculous holy object—but *Graol* can also mean noise and riot, wrath and unrest (as above).
- *Grail* forms part of the French pair *sang royal*, which means royal blood, and which is also known as *saint gral* and *sangréal*.
- *Grail* is connected to the Celtic word *dysgl* according to some researchers, which refers to a broad, deepened bowl that has the same magical characteristics as the Grail.

The Holy Grail's supernatural powers

The following overall view of the Grail and its powers emerges from the various literary sources of the Middles Ages that take up the Grail as their theme:
- It provides food in the form of a Communion wafer to the Fisher King and/or the Grail King. This not only keeps him alive, but also strengthens him, as described by Chrétien de Troyes.
- For Wolfram von Eschenbach, angels brought the Grail to earth. It also provides food and drink, enhances strength, and restores youth. A dove places a Communion wafer on the Grail, which is its source of miraculous power. This Grail has a cosmic origin. It is a thing from the stars or a meteorite with the inscription *lapis exillis* (*stone of the stars*).
- Robert de Boron's version of the legend informs the reader that Joseph of Arimathea had been fed by the Grail, or the Communion wafer, for forty long years while he was in prison in Jerusalem.
- In *Perlesvaus* it can be read that visibly fresh blood from the crucified Jesus flows from the lance of Longinus into the Grail. The forms of a child and the crucified Jesus appear in the Grail, according to the *Perlesvaus*.
- According to the Vulgate Cycle, when Nascien the Jew looked at the Grail, he went blind. Through the blood of the lance, he was able to see again. The Grail also healed a king of leprosy, and Lancelot believed he could see three figures hovering above it.
- In *Le Roman de l'Estoire dou Graal*, the Grail appeared at the royal court where it healed sick knights. No sinful person could approach it.
- In *Peredur*, a plate bearing a severed head—which was the locus of special powers, according to the Celtic faith—replaced the Grail.

A Roman soldier and his lance are also part of the mystery of the Grail. Mentioned along with the Communion wafer and the Grail chalice is the wound-healing lance of the Roman Captain Longinus, eternally dripping with the blood of the Savior.

RICHARD WAGNER AND THE GRAIL

The motive of the Grail for Richard Wagner

Through his operas *Lohengrin* (1850) and *Parsifal* (1882), the celebrated poet-composer Richard Wagner (1813–1883) has been formative for the Grail tradition of the past 125 years. With these two operas, the subject of the Grail was reestablished in the public mind during the nineteenth century. Richard Wagner had long been fascinated by Wolfram von Eschenbach's *Parzifal*. Indeed, the "Parzival Author" was even given a role in Wagner's opera *Tannhäuser*, which premiered in 1845, followed five years later by *Lohengrin*. This opera tells the story of the Grail knight who came from the heavenly City of the Grail into the world of mortals to help bring victory to the side of truth.

Lohengrin, son of Percival

The Grail knight Lohengrin, about whom the audience discovers little, comes to the aid of Elsa of Brabant in a power struggle. Lohengrin appears to Elsa in a dream and saves her. However, if he is to continue as ruler of Brabant and be Elsa's husband, she must never ask him about his name or origin. Unfortunately, other aspirants to the throne stir up doubts in Elsa about the noble birth of her future husband, and on their wedding night she asks the forbidden question. Since Elsa has trusted a sinister rumor more than Lohengrin himself, he leaves her. Only then do the people of Brabant realize that Lohengrin is the son of Percival. As Lohengrin explains to the mortals:

> In a distant land, unapproachable to your steps,
> lies a castle called Montsalvat;
> within it stands a gleaming temple
> whose like for splendor is unknown on earth;
> therein is kept as the holiest of treasures
> a vessel blessed with miraculous powers ...

Parsifal, the German Grail opera

By his own report, Wagner conceived the idea for *Parsifal* on the morning of Good Friday in 1857. But it was not until July 26, 1882 that *Parsifal* was launched at Bayreuth. The composer built his narrative around the ailing Grail King Amfortas. Amfortas was the son of the first Grail King, Titurel. Many years previously, he had sallied out armed with the Holy Spear intending to put an end to the sorcery of Klingsor. Klingsor had an enchanted garden of love where, with the assistance of beautiful maidens, he sought to seduce the Knights of the Grail into breaking their vow of chastity. Amfortas failed: in the embrace of a "woman of fearsome beauty" he forgot his mission and, in his intoxication, dropped the spear—which Klingsor stole and, laughing maniacally, plunged it into Amfortas' heart. Amfortas suf-

Richard Wagner was fascinated by the Grail legend. For him it was connected with release from earthly suffering and entering a better world. In his *Parsifal*, Wagner presents a man who learns through suffering.

fered yet from this wound. It would never heal until rescue should come through a "pure fool," who was "by compassion made wise."

Wagner and the Grail legend

For Wagner, the Grail was not a stone (as it had been for Wolfram von Eschenbach) but rather the well known, miraculous, life-giving vessel. The Grail fed all pure knights with the power of eternal life; those who approached it in sin would incur eternal agony, as demonstrated by Amfortas' wound. However, Wagner also saw the Grail as a symbol for the renewal of art in society. This richly stratified artistic presentation of the Grail motive fascinated King Ludwig II of Bavaria (1845–1886), who disguised himself as Lohengrin; and turned his Schloss Neuschwanstein into the Temple of the Grail. Among the watercolors in his Schloss Berg at Lake Starnberger, Ludwig commissioned one of the Grail as a blue bowl.

Wagner's operas are also enjoyed outside Europe, as here in San Francisco in 1978. This is a scene from *Lohengrin*, in which the swan knight with his superhuman nature assists in mortal matters.

Max Bruckner designed this scenery for the first act of Richard Wagner's *Parsifal* at its premiere in Bayreuth in 1882. It shows the Temple of the Grail, which is a duplicate of Siena cathedral in Italy.

THE GRAIL AND THE TAROT

The tarot deck

The tarot deck comprises 78 cards that are used for fortune telling or for help in life. Remarkably, and certainly not coincidentally, the tarot pack emerged not terribly long after the Grail legend itself, most likely in Italy, and spread rapidly from there throughout Europe during the course of the fourteenth century. The origin of the tarot deck is unclear. Some authorities believe that it arrived from India by means of Western travelers. Others take the view that the Order of the Knights Templar brought it from the Near East into Europe. Originally, there were four additional cards among the twenty-two major arcana (also called trump cards): the knights. These may have represented the Templars themselves, as they disappeared from the tarot deck some time after the Order of Knights Templar was expelled from the Church. Even so, the Church continued to abhor the cards: they were outlawed as the "Devil's Prayerbook" and condemned as a "ladder to Hell."

Feminine aspects of the tarot

One reason for the Church's proscription may be that tarot pictures are rather feminine in nature and closely connected with cyclic ideas of rebirth and spiritual renewal. Another reason may be that there is an iconographical similarity between the four aces and established symbols of the Grail. Drawing connections between these symbols and the concept of cyclical renewal of life—thus reflecting the power of the Grail by which everything is renewed and made fruitful—is diametrically opposed to the views of the Church, which holds that all of life runs a linear course and culminates in the Last Judgment. The worldview of the Church rejects belief in the archaic mother goddesses that predate the emergence of Christianity, as well as the associated belief in nature as an eternally renewing fount of youth.

Are the cards of the tarot nothing less than a veiled representation of the Grail narrative? The deck may have been devised after the Church had outlawed the Grail narrative, rejecting it as pagan.

The Tuatha de Danaan

In Chrétien de Troye's novel, four holy symbols were carried past Perceval in a procession at the City of the Grail. This was intended to help the knight and Grail-seeker become aware of the fact that he could only become the guardian of these four exceptional objects once he proved himself worthy of them. Many scholars involved in Grail research tend to see parallels between these four holy emblemata and the four magical treasures of the Tuatha de Danaan. The Tuatha de Danaan are generally understood as a legendary early

Irish people who were devoted especially to the great Irish mother goddess Danu. Their four magic treasures were the sword of Nuada, the Irish king stone *Lia Fail*, the cauldron of the Dagda, and the spear of Lugh (or Loucetios). Similarities with both the holy emblemata of the Grail and with the four suits of the tarot (wands, cups, swords, and discs) are readily apparent. Above all, one need only think of Excalibur, the famous sword of King Arthur, who proved himself worthy of that title by being the only one able to pull it from the stone.

The origin of tarot cards cannot be ascertained with certainty. The colorful cards emerged suddenly in Renaissance Italy and spread rapidly through Europe. In early variations, four knights were part of the major arcana.

The four tarot aces

William Butler Yeats (1865–1939), Irish poet and winner of the Nobel Prize for Literature, seems to have been the first to recognize the parallels between the four treasures of Tuatha de Danaan and the four aces in the tarot deck. Also hidden in the tarot aces are the four emblemata of the Holy Grail: the sword stands for King Arthur, the disc (or pentacle) in the tarot deck appears several times in the Grail legend as a platter, the cup or chalice stands for Percival, and the wand (represented in the tarot deck as a wand or flowering rod) represents the wounded Fisher King Amfortas. The wand and flowering rod symbolize fertility.

THE CHRISTIAN
GRAIL TRADITION

The vial of Saint Januarius' blood in the Naples cathedral is extraordinary. Three times a year, before the eyes of the faithful, the blood in it becomes liquid. Is this a trick? Cardinal Michele Giordano prefers to call it a miracle and holds it up with pride.

THE BLOOD OF CHRIST

The symbolism of the Holy Blood

Dietrich, the father of Philip of Flanders, for whom Chrétien de Troyes wrote his *Perceval*, is known to have "brought the Holy Blood home to Bruges from Jerusalem" in 1150 upon his return from the Second Crusade. Even today, it is still venerated there as the "Holy Blood" that poured out of Jesus on the cross. In the Catholic Church, such "blood relics" are quite common, as they make it possible for the faithful to experience an aspect of God on earth. Some, like the vial of Saint Januarius' blood in Naples, enjoy almost magical veneration.

A famous Italian blood miracle

Januarius, bishop of Benevento, was beheaded in Italy under Emperor Diocletian around 305 CE. The body and head of the bishop were venerated in various churches and monasteries. When the mortal remains of Januarius were at last laid to rest in Naples in 1497, the two parts of the corpse were buried separately. Januarius' body rests in the crypt under the cathedral, while his head is kept in a bust reliquary behind the main altar of the side chapel. At least twice a year (on September 19, his feast day, and the first Saturday in May) a ritual takes place which enthralls the faithful and the skeptical alike. Two vials containing the outpoured blood of the saint are brought near to the head, and after a time the blood becomes liquid again. The liquification of the blood is visible proof of the fact that Januarius is not dead, but alive in the next world. This miracle confirms eternal life, as it represents the continuity in a symbolic way.

The Grail in southern Germany

In Weingarten, Germany another story is told of the blood of Jesus, in which the Roman soldier Longinus plays a completely different role. In fact, according to this legend, Longinus gathered up the earth of Golgotha that was soaked the blood of the crucified Christ. This earth appeared later in the Italian city of Mantua, where after some peregrination it came into the possession of Judith, Countess of Flanders and wife of Welf IV. From her death bed on the day after Ascension Day in 1094 CE, Judith bequeathed the reliquary to Weingarten Abbey, the family seat and burial place of the Welfs.

Every Ascension Day in Weingarten, a *Blutritt*, or "blood ride," takes place, a ritual whose origins are obscure. The first written record comes from the year 1529, which refers to the blood ride as an old established custom. The tradition reached its peak in 1753, when over 7,000 riders participated in the event. Weingarten's equestrian procession is an annual article of faith made by about 3,000 riders, priests, ministers, and musical troupes, plus about 30,000 pilgrims, all of whom pray for the blessing of the holy blood.

Transubstantiation of bread and wine

In the Roman Catholic Mass, the bread or Communion wafer is materially transformed into the body of Christ. The same thing happens with the wine, which is materially transformed into the blood of Christ. However, the bread and wine retain their color, taste, and weight afterwards. In the Lateran Council of 1215, this credo was elevated to a dogma of faith: the Savior, physically present, is given in the Eucharist. Thus the Grail cup is the chalice of the Mass.

Saint Januarius experienced a gruesome death, which is not atypical for many saints. He was beheaded, as seen in this engraving of 1700. He lived in the firm faith that eternal life in God would continue after earthly death.

Blood as a divine substance

For many peoples, blood was and still is considered the vehicle of life. Blood has often been represented by symbolic materials whose colors resemble it, such as red ocher. Ancient runes were magically animated both by blood and by the color red. In many ancient religions and cults, blood was the divine element of life that is at work within people. Therefore it could only be poured after being specially prepared—in effect, it had to be the blood of a victim. Blood was also seen as the bearer of magic powers, and as food reserved exclusively for the supernatural spirits. Terms such as blood relative, blood revenge, blood lust, blood brotherhood, and the martyrs' baptism of blood all convey this now forgotten meaning. The blood sacrifice was consumed in rituals such as the Roman cult of Mithras, to shift the participants into an ecstatic state. In the Eucharist, the congregants are imbued with the cleansing and redeeming power of the holy blood.

In the Middle Ages, especially strong miraculous powers were attributed to the blood of Christ. Like that divine essence so assiduously sought by the alchemists in their laboratories, it was thought to ward off disease and even death. One drop of the Savior's blood was sufficient, according to Saint Bernard of Clairvaux, to redeem the whole world. This belief in the healing power of the Savior's blood is at the very heart of the legend of Joseph of Arimathea and all the Grail romances.

Grail blood as blood line

With his novel *The Da Vinci Code*, former English teacher Dan Brown managed to create a contemporary

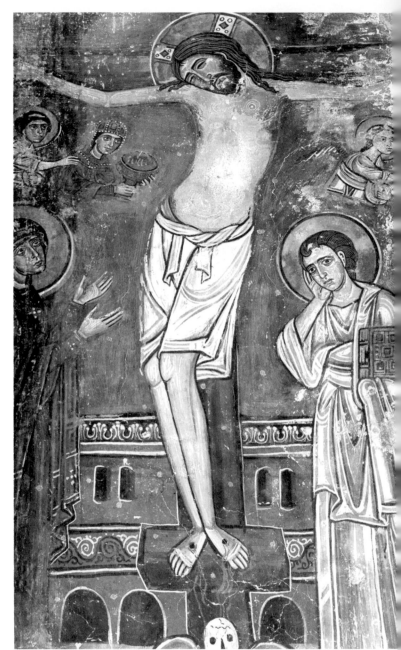

Jesus' blood flowed at the crucifixion. To the faithful, this is the blood of the Savior, who is the son of God. In that light, his blood (which was gathered in a vessel) is an imperishable divine essence that has the power to work miracles.

The blood of the crucified Jesus in *Le Morte d'Arthur*

Sir Thomas Malory (1405–1471) wrote *Le Morte d'Arthur* (*The Death of King Arthur*) ca.1469. In this tale of King Arthur and his round table, Sir Galahad sees the ailing king, who wants to die. But Galahad goes to the lance of Longinus, dips his fingers in the eternally fluid blood of the crucified Jesus, and spreads it on the king's limbs. The king is able to stand instantly and is healed.

quest for the Grail that profoundly shook the very foundations of Christianity, sending traditional historical assumptions reeling in the process. One issue in particular piqued the curiosity of contemporary readers, and at the same time stimulated vehement protests from churches: the question of whether Jesus of Nazareth and Mary Magdalen had children, whose descendants may still be alive in the world today (Dan Brown based this heretical thesis on the research and findings of other authors). This interpretation would recast the holy blood of the Grail as a blood line. The holy blood was no longer the sacrificial blood of Jesus, but the lineage of his physical children, the fruit of his marriage to Mary Magdalen. Thus the Grail became Mary Magdalen's womb.

Clues from the Apocrypha

The Apocryphal Gospels add a great deal of tinder to this volatile pile. They are called Apocryphal because the Church rejected them centuries ago as inaccurate and inauthentic, so they do not belong to the canon of recognized Biblical texts. Passages can be found in these Apocryphal Gospels stating that Jesus loved Mary Magdalen more than the other disciples, and that he often kissed her on the lips. He entrusted secrets to her, and Peter protested particularly angrily about this. Many people called Jesus *rabbi*, although Jewish custom at that time would not apply that title to an unmarried man. So whose wedding was being celebrated at Caana? Could it possibly have been that of Jesus and Mary Magdalen? Dan Brown argues that in Leonardo da Vinci's famous painting of the Last Supper, it is not John the Divine who is seated at Jesus' side, but Mary Magdalen. So, can we really derive *sang réal* (royal blood) from *saint graal* (holy grail)— or is this merely a clever play on words? Even after all these centuries, that question can still not be satisfactorily answered.

The Wedding at Caana. Some scholars suggest that Jesus and Mary Magdalen may have been the wedding celebrants on this occasion.

The sensational film *The Da Vinci Code* was produced in 2006. In his best-seller of the same name, author Dan Brown took up the thesis that the Grail represents the blood line of Jesus—and that Jesus' descendants continue to live in the world today.

There is a striking parallel between Christ on the cross and the Celtic god Lugh (or Loucetios), who also hung on the "tree" (a term by which the cross is also known). Both were pierced in the side by a lance, and like Jesus, Lugh arose from the dead.

THE SPEAR AND THE CHALICE

The Celtic and Christian origins of the spear and the chalice

The spear plays quite an important part in the Grail stories. It also has a long tradition in Celtic hero poems. Celtic warriors were masterful spear handlers: once thrown it rarely missed its goal. Furthermore, the Celtic god of light, Lugh, was pierced in the side by a spear in the same way as Jesus at the crucifixion. Lugh—and also the Germanic god Odin—were hanged on the tree of life in a similar way to Jesus on the cross. All aspired to be victims of death and then to rise again.

By 1200 CE, when the Grail romances were written, the spear (a light weapon for throwing) would already have been abandoned as a war weapon to be replaced by the lance. The lance (a heavy spear for thrusting) was used by the knight, who proved his skillful and safe handling of it at every tournament, so that it became a symbol of knightly virtue and the indication of a challenge.

As described in the Grail legend, anyone pierced by a Celtic spear immediately sank to the ground, and they could neither live nor die afterwards. For the Christian authors of the Middle Ages, the spear and the chalice were closely interconnected. This is because the Roman Captain Longinus took his spear and pierced Jesus in the side on the cross, which was the ultimate proof of Christ's death. The Bible states that blood and water flowed from the victim's resultant wound. This outflow was then caught in a chalice, according to the legend, by Joseph of Arimathea. The spear and chalice (or Grail) therefore cannot be separated from each other in the tradition of salvation (that is, of death and resurrection).

Some Celtic gods' cauldrons

The Dagda was an Irish god who possessed a cauldron, an immense and inexhaustible tureen. No one arose from it unsated. On the other hand, the cauldron of the Welsh god Diwrnach gave the best morsels of meat to the bravest warriors. Various other sacred cauldrons exist in the Celtic tradition, including one in which the hero is dipped for healing. Cormac's cauldron broke into three pieces whenever lies were spoken over it, and was completely restored as soon as three truths were uttered. The cauldron of the great goddess Ceridwen made people omniscient if they were dipped into the potion contained in it.

The legendary king of the Britons, Bran, possessed a magic cauldron capable of raising fallen warriors back to life—as illustrated on the well-known (Celtic) Gundestrup cauldron. But the resurrected warriors all shared one trait: they could not speak. This was to prevent them from telling living people about Otherworld. King Bran's magic cauldron would break if a living person was put into it.

The thirteen treasures of Britain
The thirteen legendary treasures of Britain were in the care of the wizard Merlin, and have come to be regarded as pure fiction. But among these pieces was a certain *dysgl*, which was once associated with Rhyderch, king of Strathclyde. This *dysgl* is described as "a broad, deepened dish with magical properties: … any meal desired would appear in it immediately." The grail procession described by Chrétien de Troyes fulfilled a very similar function for the guests.

Celtic cauldron and Christian Eucharist
In the Christian tradition, the magic cauldron of Celtic lore is reduced to a bowl or chalice. In the Communion rite, the cup contains wine that stands for the blood of Jesus. On the cross, Jesus' blood was poured out as a blood sacrifice for the redemption of all humankind. These ideas meld with the Celtic tradition in the perception of the Grail as a nourishing and healing vessel. The quest for the Grail and its secret, such as the knights of King Arthur's round table undertake, is a quest for a life-giving and life-receiving vessel—both protective and nurturing, like a mother's body or womb.

"The bread is the body of Christ and the chalice is the blood of Christ," said the great Church father Augustine (354–430 CE), thus emphasizing their oneness. The Grail symbolizes both: chalice and eternal food all in one.

JOSEPH OF ARIMATHEA, THE FIRST GUARDIAN OF THE GRAIL

Who was Joseph of Arimathea?

The Jewish elder Joseph of Arimathea seems to have played an important part in the life of Jesus. He may, in fact, have had the dead Jesus taken down from the cross in order to bury him in a grave originally intended for himself. All four Gospels report that Joseph of Arimathea was a wealthy man and a secret disciple of Jesus, and that it was he who sought Pilate's permission to remove the crucified Jesus from the cross. The Apocryphal Gospel of Nicodemus, which was developed during the fourth century CE and was never officially recognized by the Church, goes on to say that Nicodemus arrived with an unguent of myrrh and aloe to embalm Jesus' body. When it was discovered on Easter morning that the body of Jesus had disappeared from the grave, Joseph of Arimathea was suspected of having something to do with this, and

the henchmen of the authorities in Jerusalem arrested him and flung him into prison. According to his own report, he was freed from there by the risen Jesus.

The first Grail community around Joseph of Arimathea

Joseph had to leave Judea. With him went his sister Enygeus, her husband Bron, and other people whose names are not given. All honored the Holy Grail. This community established itself in the south of Britain in the region of Glastonbury. There, Joseph built the Lady Chapel (said to be the first church in western Europe). The story relates that a voice from the Grail spoke to them every day, making the accusation that some among them nursed guilty, carnal desires. Joseph therefore made a communal dinner table as a reminder of the Last Supper. Bron had caught a single fish that

Joseph and the Holy Grail
The Apocryphal Gospel of Nicodemus and the story of Joseph of Arimathea contained in it seems to have been the main source for Robert de Boron's work. De Boron wrote that Joseph stood under the cross and caught the blood of Christ in a chalice. Joseph had a small altar in his house which held two lighted candles and the chalice containing the blood of the Savior, and he would pray before it every day. After his release from prison Joseph left the country. With Nicodemus and a few friends, they set off onboard ship and took the chalice with the blood of Christ to far-away Britain. The little community was supplied with meals by the Grail. In this way, Joseph of Arimathea became the first Keeper of the Grail.

The Grail narrative is inconceivable without the mysterious Joseph of Arimathea. Why did he, of all people, catch the blood of Jesus at the crucifixion? Why would he have taken the body of Jesus from the cross and placed it in his own family grave?

satisfied everyone's hunger—but would not feed sinners. Those sinners had to leave the community. As time went by, Enygeus and her husband Bron had twelve children. One of these, Alein, became the future Keeper of the Grail. Before that, Joseph of Arimathea had transferred the Grail to his brother-in-law and initiated him into the secret message of Christ, which had been entrusted to him in the prison near Jerusalem by the risen Christ.

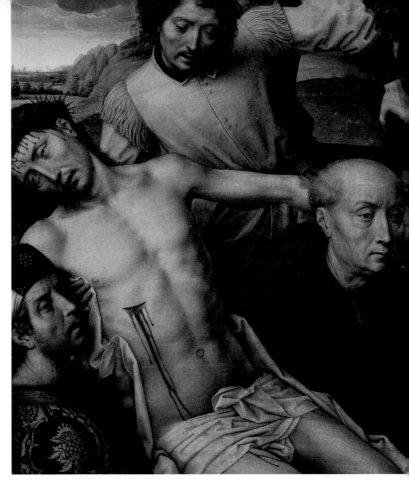

Jesus died on the cross and was then taken down from it. Blood flowed from the wound caused by the spear-thrust. Joseph of Arimathea had the abused body medically treated (the Bible mentions herbs and unguents).

What is the mystery of the Grail?

The crucial question is, into what secret or mysteries was Joseph initiated by Jesus? It is said that Jesus entrusted the Grail chalice to him as a healing vessel with the words, "as a symbol of my death." This expression is intriguing, as it recalls the Celtic cauldron of plenty, which represents the eternal cycle of life and death. The mystery of that cauldron is that everything which dies is born again, and in the Gospel of John (12:24) it is written that the kernel of wheat will bear fruit only if it dies. Thus it may be inferred that the Lord's secret words to Joseph concerned this mystery.

Joseph of Arimathea is believed to have come to Glastonbury bringing the blood shed by Jesus as he died on the cross. The research of scholars such as Laurence Gardner indicates a date of 49 CE for this event.

The Fisher King as Keeper of the Grail

The Christian roots of the Fisher King

Wolfram von Eschenbach's Parzival encountered the ailing Fisher King in his City of the Grail. The king, whose name was Amfortas, was seeking a successor.

In the Grail sagas, Cundrie is portrayed as an unbelievably hideous messenger. Wagner, in contrast, makes her seductive. Cundrie cursed Parzival for failing to ask the king the correct question.

From Wolfram, the reader learns that the old king, *le rois Peschierre* (Fisher King), was wounded by a javelin, or throwing spear, between the hips. It had become impossible for him to ride his horse, and the only amelioration of his suffering came from fishing in a small boat on a lake near his castle. In this instance, the fish stands for Christ and is symbolically connected with renewal and rebirth. The early Christians read the Greek formula for the nature of Christ as *Iesus CHristos THeou Yios Soter* (Jesus Christ God's Son Savior), whose initials form the acronym *ichthys*. In Greek, *ichthys* means fish. The fish thus became the insignia of the Christians in ancient Rome.

What is the illness that the Fisher King suffers in the Grail legend? The expression "between the hips" is generally understood to indicate an injury to the reproductive organs. In this state, the king is barren and must wait for a successor to release him. He can no longer take part in the cycle of life, according to the Celts' understanding. Similar stories of wounded kings can also be found in the old Irish *echtrai*.

The Fisher King's barren wasteland

One aspect of the mystery surrounding the ailing Fisher King and the connection between the Grail and the bleeding lance is the country that he governs, which has become a barren wilderness. What lies behind this idea? It appears in all of the Grail narratives, and Wolfram von Eschenbach strengthens it further by the appearance of the terrible Cundrie. This abysmally loathsome woman, as the poet writes, cursed Parzival, who did not manage to ask the correct questions of the Fisher King. Because of his failure, according to Cundrie, the land would be even further devastated and uninhabitable. The Celts saw Cundrie as a "pitch-black witch." Her presence augered evil and reminded people to do what is right. A few scholars, such as Jessie Weston of Great Britain and

An image of the Fisher King in the little church of Mensano. References to aspects of the Grail can be found remarkably often in and near churches, especially in Italy.

the German Hubert Lampo, interpret the figure of Cundrie in Christian-esoteric terms. They believe that there was a secret esoteric society in the Middle Ages that circulated ancient religious knowledge and esoteric wisdom in order to point out the important connections between life and death, humans and nature. Clearly, they would have believed these ideas threatened by Church dogma.

Abusing the earth

These secret societies found the Biblical mandate to "fill the earth and subdue it" (Genesis 1:28) to be fatal, as this could damage the equilibrium between man and nature. According to Lampo and Weston, these esoteric circles influenced authors such as Chrétien *et al* with their ideas of the Grail and a mystery connected to it. Author Hubert Lampo believes that the Grail was a ritual vessel, while the real mystery is hidden in "lost background information." In his opinion, this mystery concerns the polarizing forces of life and death and human's abuse of nature. The Fisher King's barren country is thus a warning that has validity even today.

Parzival and the dying Amfortas. The precise illness that afflicts the Fisher King is obscure.

Was the wedding at Caana, at which Jesus transformed water into wine, the wedding of Mary Magdalen and Jesus? Why else would his mother Mary say to the servants, "do as he bids you" (John 2:5) if he was not the bridegroom?

MARY MAGDALEN, VESSEL OF GOD

The mystery of Mary Magdalen

The risen Jesus appeared first to Mary Magdalen, who may be the woman in Mark's Gospel out of whom he drove seven devils (Mark 16:9). Who was this woman?

There is little to read about her in the Gospels, and yet Jesus chose to appear to her first of all. Mary Magdalen is a motive in many medieval images, where she is frequently shown in a long red gown with golden blonde hair and a beautiful face—and occasionally also topless. She is nearly always found standing at the foot of the cross on which Jesus hangs. This Mary of Magdala is known by Christians as a penitent sinner, and by Gnostics as the Lord's beloved. This beautiful tear-stained penitent is present in many French churches. Further, despite the scarcity of her name in Biblical contexts, she designates a particular Neolithic period, the Magdalenian (La Madeleine being the site of crucial archaeological finds in the Dordogne). In addition, an island north of Sardinia bears her name, as do colleges in Oxford and Cambridge, and mountain ranges in northern and southern Italy.

A perplexing statement

A mystifying comment is attributed to René of Anjou, who is said to have possessed a reproduction of the authentic Grail chalice. As early as the Middle Ages, René of Anjou also saw a relationship between the Magdalen and the Grail. Two sentences were engraved on King René of Anjou's Grail chalice:

Whoso drinks me
God shall see.
Whoso at one good breath drains me
Shall God and the Magdalen see!

What did the king mean mean to convey in these sentences? Was Mary Magdalen in fact truly seen as the first among the apostles, because Jesus trusted her more than the others, as can be learned in the Gospel of Mary?

The hidden gospels

In 1945, Egyptians working in fields near Nag Hammadi in central Egypt discovered a sealed jug containing the first of several important Gnostic texts found nearby. Among these was the Gospel (or Book) of Thomas, the Gospel of Mary (Magdalen), the Gospel of Philip and others, all of which shed much light on early Christian religious beliefs. The Church had rejected these texts from its official canon very early on, as they were held to contain errant teachings with Gnostic leanings. Gnostics believed that a demiurge, or secondary god, had created the world, and that Jesus never physically died on the cross. The Nag Hammadi texts make it clear that there was a circle of women around Jesus. This supports the Bible's representation of Mary Magdalen at the cross and at the empty tomb of Jesus. Furthermore, the Gnostic texts also teach that it was Mary Magdalen that Jesus chose as his successor, rather than Peter, the fisherman.

René of Anjou, Duke of Calabria and Lorraine, Duke of Anjou, and King of Naples was a respected artist, writer, musician, and tournament architect who was fascinated by the Grail legend.

Mary Magdalen and the *Last Supper*

Dan Brown, author of *The Da Vinci Code*, was not the first person who has claimed to have discovered Mary Magdalen in Leonardo da Vinci's well-known *Last Supper* fresco. Other authorities, such as Jean Markale, had already considered this possibility many years earlier. Could it be true that in da Vinci's brilliant fresco the figure to Jesus' right (whom art historians identify as the favorite disciple, John) is actually a woman? It is certainly worth noting this figure's graceful hands, the refined face, the feminine chest, and the gold neckline of the robe he or she wears. In addition, there are interesting correspondences between this person's clothing and that of Jesus (whom the great Italian artist called "the Savior" in his notes). Jesus is depicted wearing a red robe and a blue mantle, while the disciple immediately to his right wears a blue robe and a red mantle.

The suggestive M

Even the spatial arrangement of this pair of figures produces a significant shape, a great M—as if Leonardo da Vinci sought to give further confirmation of the person he had depicted here. Did the sly Leonardo seek to state his personal conviction about the relationship between Mary Magdalen and Jesus in this fresco of the Last Supper? It is commonly thought that he created the fresco expressly in order to relay some secret message. But what that message is has not been unraveled. Some scholars believe that the artist sought to express the preeminent status of astrology at the time through the *Last Supper*. The twelve apostles would symbolize the different signs of the zodiac, among whom John (or Mary Magdalen, as preferred) would represent the sign of Libra, his (or her) hands laid symbolically one on top of the other in a symbolic gesture of sensitive weighing and reconciliation.

Leonardo da Vinci's *Last Supper* shows Jesus with the dish that many scholars see as the true Grail. Whether the figure beside him is actually Mary Magdalen or John remains a matter of dispute.

Why Mary Magdalen?

Some esoteric theories state that only Mary Magdalen knew the true secrets of Jesus' teachings. Unknown to his disciples, he revealed all of his mysteries to her, or at least the Gnostic texts seem to make this assumption. What obscure mystery surrounded Mary Magdalen and Jesus, to which Leonardo wanted to direct our attention (albeit cryptically)? She is seen as a whore, although this is an ancient symbolic meaning. In the original Temple of Jerusalem that Solomon built in the east of the city, the triune goddess Mari-Anna-Ishtar, the Great Whore of Babylon, was revered along with her savior-son, Tammuz (Ezekiel 8:14). Ishtar was the Whore of Babylon, and her name is even more significant because it means "woman (*ish* or *esh[e]t*) of the [Babylonian] tower (*tar*)." Magdalen is also a translation of "woman of the towered temple," so that her name points to the temple of the Great Whore of Babylon, which had three towers. In her book *The Woman's Encyclopedia of Myths and Secrets*, Barbara Walker mentions another parallel: the dead savior of the Ishtar cult can only be seen by women at first, and

The well-known scene from the New Testament in which Mary Magdalen washes Jesus' feet and dries them with her long hair suggests to many modern scholars that she was his loving wife.

Mary Magdalen was the first to see the risen Jesus. From these considerations, Walker deduces her theory of the symbolic equivalence of the Magdalen and the Babylonian Ishtar, the Great Whore (who, of course, could never have been formally accepted in that form by Christianity). Walker's ideas explain the name and great significance of Mary Magdalen for Jesus' inner circle, at least.

A certain ritual

According to some sources, a ritual with a deadly end was part of the worship of the Great Whore. Male victims were baptized by the priestesses before they descended to the underworld. In the Gospel of Mathew, this is how Jesus explains Mary Magdalen's gift to him when she bathed his feet: "In pouring this ointment on my body she has done it to prepare me for burial." (Mt 26:7–12). Does this suggest a close ritual connection between Jesus and Mary? The red gown that was worn by the Whore of Babylon, too, is frequently shown on Mary Magdalen in medieval art, marking her as a sinner.

It is generally accepted that Magdalen derives from a place called Magdala, a fishing town. Because the root word *migdal* means "tower," church towers were often associated with the Magdalen.

THE TEMPLARS, GUARDIANS AND POSSESSORS OF THE GRAIL?

The Temple Brothers in Arms

It is frequently repeated that the medieval Order of the Templars was immeasurably wealthy and that it was in possession of the Grail. Originally known as the Order (or Knights) of the Temple, and also calling themselves the Brothers in Arms of the Temple, for the first ten years of their existence they wore rags and cast-offs in place of fine clothing. This knightly order flourished from the start: in 1119, nine Frankish knights were based in Jerusalem, and after their recognition by the pope at the Council of Troyes in 1127, there were already 300 brothers ranked among the Templars. The rapid ascendancy of the new order was particularly spurred on by the support of the charismatic ecclesiastic Bernard of Clairvaux.

The four Templar classes

The Order consisted of four classes: (1) the knights, *fratres milites* (fighting brothers), who initially were required to be of noble origin, (2) the chaplains, or *fratres capellani* (praying brothers), the spiritual elite who preserved the Order's secret knowledge, (3) the squires and heralds, or *fratres servientes* (serving brothers), who wore black mantles, and (4) the domestics, agricultural workers, servants and craftsmen, the *fratres famuli et officii* (working brothers), who wore brown or blue livery. The craftsmen were further organized in relation to their status as freemen (master builders, masons, and stone cutters), vassals (joiners and locksmiths), and masters of the axe (carpenters). The chaplains and the knights together formed the heart of the Knights Templar. The knights' weapons were decorated with symbols of the Kabbalah, an esoteric knowledge that they guarded.

Jacques de Molay was the last Grand Master of the Knights Templar before the Order was crushed by Philip the Fair of France. In 1314, the Grand Master was burned at the stake in Paris.

A highly influential order

The Templars were privileged from the beginning. They were exempted from tithes (taxes), even permitted to raise tithes themselves from time to time, and were almost always to keep all their booty of war. Many nobles left their income to the Templars or bequeathed their land to the Order.

At the beginning of the thirteenth century, the Order could mobilize over 30,000 knights. Its sphere of influence stretched from France, where it originated, through Germany, England, Spain, Portugal, Italy, the Balkans, and of course to Palestine. The Order of armed brothers thus became the most powerful institution of the Middle Ages. The Templars were at the forefront of many important political decisions, and their wealth tipped the scales on more than one occasion. In time they became extremely wealthy financiers, although they themselves were committed to simple clothing and an ascetic lifestyle.

International cash transfers

When it became clear how well the Order understood wealth management, kings and popes alike entrusted the Templars with the administration of real estate properties, tax receipts, gold, cash, and jewels. Their banking business flourished. Indeed, there is some justification for crediting the Templars with the invention of the checking account. The opening of bank accounts, disbursement of pensions and annuities, loans, endorsements, pawn brokering, bill collection, international money transfers, and guarantees were all part of their highly specialized business. Anyone depositing funds for safekeeping in Paris or London could by exchange get their money back in any currency in Jerusalem or Greece. Checks and letters of exchange were invented by the Templars, who also took charge of investment advice for the European monarchy and traders.

The Knights Templar were originally established to protect Christian pilgrims, but they rose rapidly to become an exceptionally powerful institution. The Templars' insignia was a red cross worn on the left shoulder.

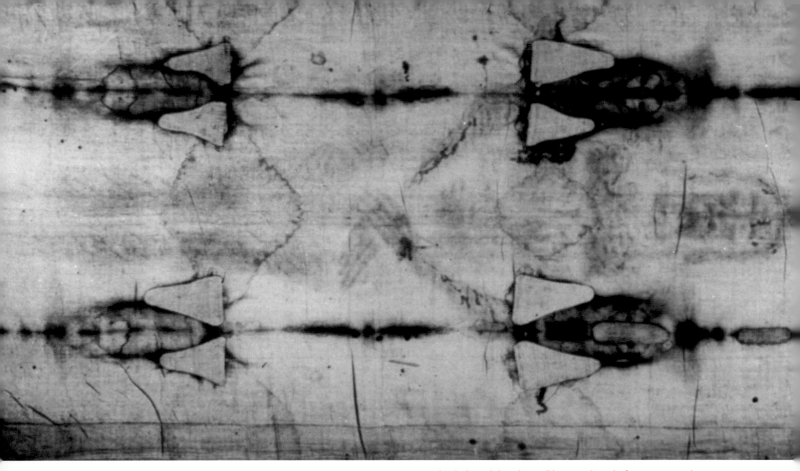

It is also believed that the well-known Shroud of Turin was in the Templars' possession for a time. Recently it has been suggested that the image on the cloth is that of the last Grand Master of the Templars, Jacques de Molay.

The backlash against the brothers in arms

The Templars initiated the construction of a number of important cathedrals and achieved truly amazing results in the field of architecture. The Spanish churches built by the Templars are characterized by a marvelous synthesis of Gothic and Oriental architectural elements.

There are no reliable figures for the Templar fortune at the point in time when the pope and king turned against them. One reason it is so difficult to come to an accurate estimate of the total assets of the Knights Templar is that it is not clear whether they themselves always gave an accurate figure for their income. In any case, on a Friday 13th in the year 1307, Philip the Fair of France and Pope Clement VI had all of the Templars arrested. The king wanted to get his hands on their enormous fortune, and the pope accused them of heresy and thus of betraying Christianity.

Baphomet and other offenses

The pope's accusation of heresy was primarily based on the Templars' veneration of a strange head that they called Baphomet. The meaning of this name is unknown. Most scholars take the view that Baphomet is a parody of the name Mohammed. During the trial of the Templars, the brothers were questioned individually and the information they gave about Baphomet was highly contradictory. Some Templars described the head as white and bearded, others as red. Yet others associated it with a cat that could speak, and a further group called it "Old Goat." The head itself was not found among the Templars, but one head was found with the inscription *Caput LVIII M*—the meaning of which remains unclear even today. The remaining charges of heresy also remain unconfirmed today. Did the Templars indeed spit on the cross as accused? Did they deny the resurrection of Jesus? What form did their allegedly blasphemous faith really take?

It is undeniable that strange heads can be found at known Templar churches. This head cult remains an enigma, as no one knows what Baphomet actually looked like.

in southern France, they are believed to have been guardians of an ancient treasure that was originally taken as booty by the Roman emperor Titus when he took Jerusalem in 70 AD and which the western Goths later stole from Rome. This was the treasure of the Temple of Jerusalem, which included the seven-armed candelabra (the Menorah), as well as jewels and gold.

And what about the Grail? Scratched into a wall of the castle at Domme in the French Dordogne, where seventy Templars were arrested between 1307 and 1318, is a graffiti showing a remarkable crucifixion scene. Departing from tradition, it shows Joseph of Arimathea catching the blood of Jesus in a bowl as it flows from the wound in his side while to the left stands a scantily clothed woman holding an object in her hand. This is probably Mary Magdalen, since she is associated with both the Templars and the Grail. At the Templar church of Sta Maria Maggiore in Bologna, Italy, a Templar lord, Peter de Rotis (who died at the beginning of the thirteenth century), holds up a cup—could this be a representation of the Grail?

The Templars and the Holy Grail

One fact about the Order is never disputed, however. The Templars were always on the lookout for treasures of any kind. This applied to material property as well as precious reliquaries such as the heads of saints (including those of the apostles), the Shroud of Turin, the Ark of the Covenant, and the Holy Grail. In their spiritual homeland, the Languedoc-Roussillon region

An interpretation of the Grail

In his book on the Templars (published in 1860), Ferdinand Wilcke gave a remarkable interpretation for the word *graal*. He saw the term as originating from the Hebrew, and translatable as "precious legacy." According to Wilcke, *graal* comes from the mystical Jewish Kabbalah, which attempts to reveal the secrets of God. The author interpreted the chalice of the Grail as the precious legacy of the Last Supper.

On the grim morning of October 13, 1307, Pope Clement V had every Templar in France, Italy, and Spain arrested. He waited until March 22, 1312 to dissolve the Order and to condemn Jacques de Molay, the last Grand Master of the Knights Templar, to death at the stake.

The Grail dish
as King Herod's plate

Many Templar scholars interpret the appearance of the Grail, as the Templars themselves imagined it, in connection with the figure of John the Baptist. He was revered by the Templars as a forerunner of Jesus and because he baptized the emergent Messiah in the River Jordan. At Salome's behest, John the Baptist was beheaded at the court of King Herod. His head was then presented to Salome on a plate, or chalice-like paten. John had died for his faith. The Templars honored him for this with a chalice which they made the emblem of their Johannine spiritual federation. A little-known document reflects this credo. It contains the passage, *I believe in the one God and I revere John the Baptist, who performed no miracles ...*

Detail of a fresco from the Carolingian period showing the head of John the Baptist on a chalice. The forerunner of Jesus, as he called himself, baptized the savior in the River Jordan. He was executed on King Herod's orders.

Portugal, land of The Grail?

Portugal is rich and interesting terrain for Templar scholars. In the first place, the Regent Teresa had already conferred possession of properties to the Templars on March 19, 1128, including the fortress of Soure in the northern part of the country, i.e., prior to the Council of Troyes in 1129. This in itself is extraordinary, since until now it has been generally assumed that between the founding of the Order in 1119 and January 13, 1129 (the date of their official recognition by the Church), the Templars had concentrated solely on their activities in Jerusalem. Secondly, and importantly, Teresa's granddaughter was designated as a "Sister of the Knights Templar" in a bill of sale. Does this prove beyond a doubt that the Order also accepted female members—and did they also recognize Mary Magdalen as a spiritual sister?

Por tuo Gral

The extent of Portugal's importance to the Knights Templar is demonstrated by a further event, which remains highly mysterious even to this day. In February of 1159, King Alfonso I of Portugal, a great friend and sponsor of the Order, bequeathed a stretch of land around Cera to the Templars that had not been populated up to that time. The document certifying this donation does not bear the usual wax seal, but a circular stamp consisting of two outer rings and an unusual chrismon, or depiction of the initials of Christ. In the outer ring is the name and title of the king: *Rex Alfonsus*. In the inner ring, his sons are recorded as witnesses of the donation: *cum filiis suis*. At the center is the chrismon, a monogram formed of the Greek initial letters of *Christos*—*X* (chi) and *P* (rho). Unusually, however, the gaps in the monogram are filled with the Latin letters *T*, *U*, *G*, *R*, and *AL*. Taken with the monogram itself, the whole can be clearly read as *Por tuo Gral* ("for your Grail"). Owing to the ambiguous placement of the *R*, however, it is also possible to read this inscription as *Portugal*, the name of the country. Since ambiguous terminology was a specialty of the Order of the Knights Templar and those associated with it, we cannot be sure which reading is the correct one. Is Portugal the Land of the Grail? It remains a mystery.

The great respect accorded to John the Baptist by the Templars is shown in a stone medallion in one of their former monasteries at Salers in the Auvergne region of France. John's head rests on a charger, gazing powerfully and forebodingly down from the vaulting.

The Grail or John's head of Salers

Salers lies in the heart of Auvergne in France, a mere 12½ miles (20 km) north of Aurillac. Every step through its narrow lanes lined with centuries-old dwellings evokes the spirit of those long-lost knights with the red flaring cross. One particularly prominent building, three stories tall and built of massive stones, is the Templar monastery built over eight hundred years ago. Those who enter the *Maison des Templiers* today are confronted with a baleful head that forms the keystone of the vaulting. Some Templar scholars understand this to be the head of John the Baptist, who is presented in a dramatically insistent way. The flame-like hair and beard and the figure's slanting eyes give the face an effortlessly commanding—if not truly demonic—expression. Just like the triune head at their Portuguese headquarters in Tomar, this head is rests on a flat, circular charger that evokes ideas of a Grail-like vessel.

Important Grail Traditions in Europe

A MYTHICAL GRAIL CASTLE

The castle of the Grail

The castle of the Grail is the temple of the Grail. Its name, Munsalvaesche (or Montsalvat), could be translated as "Mount Salvation." Munsalvaesche is an *axis mundi*, a place where heaven and earth meet. All temples and holy mountains are understood to be *axes mundi*, but only in a few cases is there real significance behind the claim. Among these are the mythical Indian Mount Meru (or Mount Sumeru) in the Urals, whose summit points directly to the pole star, the Buddhist Mount Kailash in Tibet, and Mount Golgotha in Israel, the site of the crucifixion of Jesus. But where could Mount Salvasch (or Munsalvaesche) actually be? Quite a number of Grail scholars believe it must be in the Pyrénées. They seek to connect it with Montségur of the Cathars, since the names sound similar. But Montségur translates as "safe mountain," and the Cathars certainly did not regard it as a holy place. A work long associated with Wolfram von Eschenbach, known as *The Later Titurel*, describes the mountain temple of Munsalvaesche in considerable detail as "one hundred cubits in diameter, around which stood seventy-two chapels of octagonal shape. Every two chapels had a tower six stories tall with flying staircases leading upwards."

Precious gems and crystals

With regard to the accoutrements of the temple, the poet writes of precious jewels, gold, clear crystals, and blue enamel on the dome. The guardians of Munsalvaesche were the *templeis* or "templars." It remains a vexed question whether the description really refers to the monastery of San Juan de la Peña, which is located in the Pyrénées (see pp. 74–79), since the Holy Chalice (the chalice of the Last Supper) was kept there in his lifetime. However, it is more likely that Munsalvaesche was a heavenly ideal, a refuge of salvation and everlasting peace such as mortals can only dream of.

Esclarmonde de Foix was an important Cathar woman. Cathar priests called themselves *Parfaits* (the completed ones). Priestesses (*Parfaites*) like Esclarmonde were also known as *Bonnes Dames* (good ladies).

Esclarmonde de Foix

Princess Esclarmonde (1151–1215) lived in thirteenth-century Foix, near Montségur, when the Cathars were bloodily persecuted. Even during her own lifetime she was highly respected and known as a committed Cathar. Her name means "Light of the World," which led Otto Rahn to see her as Wolfram's Grail Bearer. There are other indications in support of his thesis that Montségur was, in fact, the Grail castle of Munsalvaesche. One denizen of the fortress was named Pérelhe (in Latin: Perilla), and thus had the same name as the first Grail King in the later continuation of Wolfram von Eschenbach's *Titurel* poem. Poetic coincidence or something more? This matter, too, cannot be clearly settled.

Otto Rahn and his search for Munsalvaesche

Prominent representatives of the Third Reich were deeply infatuated with the myth of the Holy Grail, seeing in it a proto-Aryan legacy to which the general population needed to be reconnected. One person who was actively seeking the location of the Grail at that time was Otto Rahn (1904–1939). In his book *Crusade Against the Grail* (1933), he described following leads into the French Languedoc, the country of the Cathars. Rahn connected the Grail castle Munsalvaesche with the Aryan Asgard or Valhalla, and believed he recognized it in the Cathar castle of Montségur. For Rahn, the Grail was a heretical symbol that was directed precisely against Christianity. He drew this conclusion from the behavior of four daring Cathars, who on the eve of their surrender of Montségur stole out of that high mountain fortress at night by rope, carrying to safety something that could not be allowed to fall into the hands of the French forces. Rahn was convinced this was the Grail, a pagan object in direct conflict with the Christian cross.

On top of Montségur, the original fortress refuge of the Cathars floated like a ship in the mist. The ruins that remain on the site are reached by a steep, rocky footpath through brush. Climbers are rewarded at the top by a stunning view of nearby peaks in the Pyrenées.

THE SPANISH TRAIL

The Grail in the Pyrenées

Framed by the harsh, rocky outcrop of the southern face of Monte Pano on the Spanish side of the Pyrenées, north of Huesca, is the former monastery of San Juan de la Peña (St. John of the Rock). This remote spot high in the mountains was an extraordinary spiritual center in the Middle Ages that focused especially on the human quest for transformation into higher, spiritual beings. From the village of Santa Cruz de la Serós, a paved but winding road leads into the mountainous region, thickly overgrown with pines, beeches, and oaks. Almost 1300 years ago, a young nobleman named Voto was hunting in this area. His discovery was to have a significant impact on contemporary Grail scholarship.

An ancient legend

The triangle in his hands ties the legend of Juan de Atarés (see box, right) directly to that of the Salomonic

Hidden in the Pyrenées is the old monastery of San Juan de la Peña. In this place of silence built into a rocky overhang, visitors are fascinated by the graves of long gone Knights of the Grail.

A strange discovery

When a deer passed Voto, he pursued it into the dark forest on Monte Pane, straying further and further from human habitation. Suddenly his horse shied at a deep chasm and threatened to slip. In the direst peril, Voto would surely have plunged to his death over the sheer cliff had he not prayed to John the Baptist for help. His horse froze motionless at the edge of the abyss, stayed by a spiritual hand. When the hunter explored the cliff more closely, he discovered a cave in the dense underbrush. It was only with great effort that Voto could break through to it, and found a space that had been converted into a chapel. On the altar lay the uncorrupted body of a man holding a white, triangular stone in his hands. Engraved on the stone was a Latin inscription that translates as, "I, Juan de Atarés, who was the first hermit in this place (where I lived humbly for the sake of the love of God), had this church built to honor John the Baptist to the best of my ability. And here I rest. Amen."

Temple of Jerusalem. Hiram, the exquisitely skilled building master of the Temple (whom the Freemasons consider their founder) was a descendant of Tubal Cain. According to the legend, he was the first man to live in Spain. Pyrene, to whom the Pyrenées are popularly thought to owe their name, was his daughter. Shortly before the completion of his work for King Solomon in Jerusalem, Hiram's jealous assistants destroyed the molten sea, an enormous bronze basin that Hiram was creating for the Temple. In desperation, Hiram threw himself into the roaring flames and thus arrived at the underground kingdom of Tubal Cain.

The brilliant master craftsman Hiram devised a range of implements for Solomon's temple in Jerusalem, and was murdered by his own envious associates. This Hiram legend is the basis of the Freemasons.

There, Hiram received a golden triangle and a T-shaped hammer from Tubal Cain. The golden triangle was a symbol of humanity's mission to build its own temple of divine origin. The person to undertake this would find the golden triangle on the altar. Thus far the interpretation of the legend.

The development of the monastery

Voto proclaimed the location of the chapel of San Juan and quickly attracted men to follow the true example of Juan de Atarés. In time, the hermitage grew and became a monastery, whose fame and reputation spread far and wide. Even today, San Juan de la Peña remains as it originally was, completely surrounded by forest. Tucked under an overhanging rock, it clings to it like a swallow's nest, its walls washed with the rosy stain of the rock above. This magical place was founded ca. 850 CE and was developed by the hermits Marthelo and Benedicto into an important regional spiritual center under the protection of the kings of Pamplona.

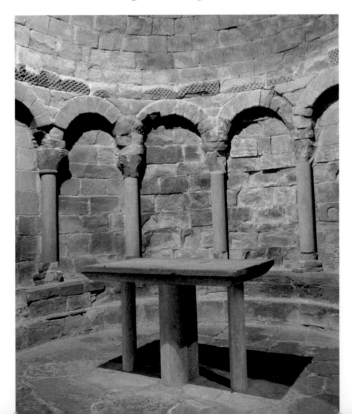

The ancient altar stone in the apse of the monastery of San Juan de la Peña. According to contemporary Grail scholars, the Knights of the Grail held sacred ceremonies in front of the Holy Chalice (or Grail chalice) here.

The wall tombs of bygone Knights of the Grail can still be seen in the monastery of San Juan de la Peña. The distinctive rose cross, to which the secret society of the Rosicrucians refers, probably finds its origin here.

The Grail at San Juan de la Peña

During the Middle Ages, a "thyngge" spread from San Juan de la Peña to distant parts of the West. This "thyngge" (called "Grail" by the noble knights) was a superbly crafted chalice cut from an emerald-green eastern agate whose surface reflects the ambient light in every color including magenta. The cup is set into a golden mount decorated with pearls, emeralds and rubies, which rests on a shallow hemispherical base of green onyx. Below the cup, its two great golden handles form a heart. This impressive chalice of Eastern origin contributed substantially to the development of the Grail legend. Though it was kept in the monastery of San Juan de la Peña for many centuries, today it is found in the chapel of the *Santo Caliz* in the Valencia cathedral. At the end of the 1950s, art historian Antonio Beltran concluded from his research that the cup of the chalice, which is made of agate, is the oldest part of the whole object and probably dates from between the fourth century BCE and the first century CE, and that it was probably made somewhere in the Near East, possibly Syria, Palestine or eastern Egypt. The base, which was once a vessel in its own right, also comes from the East and was associated with the cup during the tenth century. The chalice in its present form, he explains, is documented as early as the year 1399.

The tale of a journey

Following the crucifixion, the cup of the chalice of San Juan de la Peña arrived first in Rome, where it remained in the possession of several successive popes. In 258 CE, Pope Sixtus II entrusted it to his deacon Laurentius (or Lawrence, later Saint Lawrence) during the persecution of the Christians that took place under Emperor Valerian. Laurentius arranged for the cup to be brought to his home town, which was Huesca, in Spain. In 716, Huesca itself came under threat from the Arabs. When the bishop of Huesca realized that the precious reliquary was again in danger, he had it taken to the distant monastery of San Adrián de Sasabe in the valley of Borau. The monks there protected it from the eighth through the tenth centuries, until it was sent to the residence of the new king of Aragon in Jaca in 1063. In 1076, the bishop's seat was transferred from Jaca and Huesca to San Juan de la Peña, and thus the cup arrived at the cave monastery. The cup, which in the meantime had been reworked into a chalice, finally came to rest in the cathedral of Valencia in 1437, where it is revered as the Holy Grail to this very day.

The Rosicrucians in San Juan de la Peña

On the funerary plaques of the knights of the Order of St. John, found in the mausoleum that is known as the monastery's "Pantheon of Noble Knights," is a hermetic cross with five roselike blooms. Probably to protect the cup (or Grail) from all enemies—and especially against the evil in the world—young men had been drawn to San Juan ever since the ninth

century, where they joined the knightly order of the Brotherhood of the Knights of San Juan de la Peña. Today it is known that they underwent a baptism of fire (that is, the baptism of the Holy Spirit) in a font fed by a spring that rises within the church. As Wolfram von Eschenbach wrote in his *Parzival*, "water gives many souls such radiance that angels cannot be more bright."

The Grail formerly kept in the Pyrenéan monastery can be visited today in the cathedral of Valencia. The upper portion of the Grail (the agate cup) is the oldest.

Initiation and the baptism of fire

The baptism of fire is the process within an initiation (or induction) by which people become one with the divinity. The letters INRI, *Iesvs Nazarenvs Rex Iudaeorvm* (Jesus of Nazareth, King of the Jews) are reconceived as *Igne Natura Renovatur Integras* (All Nature is Renewed by Fire). Behind this lies the concept of the mythical bird called the phoenix, which bursts into flames when it dies, only to repeatedly be resurrected from its ashes; the phoenix is connected with the mystery of the Grail. It is not impossible that the Knights of San Juan de la Peña are the substance behind the legend of the Grail Knights. Later, authors such as Wolfram von Eschenbach and Chrétien de Troyes spread the fame of the Grail with their epic narratives.

The chrismon

On the two-tier funerary niches of the Knights of San Juan de la Peña (or Grail Knights?) is a chrismon. At San Juan, this symbols lacks any Greek or Roman letters, which are otherwise found on such images. The chrismon is a six-rayed star, and for alchemists it is a symbol of the *spiritus mundi* (world spirit) that effects the transmutation of base matter into noble matter. At the same time, it is omnipresent

The mythical bird called the phoenix ascends repeatedly from the ashes, its youth restored. Thus it became a symbol for Christ, who similarly overcame death. The Grail, too, gives new life to those who find it.

power. For the Christians, a chrismon is the monogram of Christ and was often displayed in a prominent place on a church, such as a tympanum (gable area) over a window or door. It is formed from the Greek letters *Chi* and *Rho*, which are the initial letters of Christ and stand for the Savior. The traditional interpretation of the chrismon reads *XR AO*, which may be understood as *Christ est alpha et omega* (Christ is the beginning and the end). Read in horizontal layers, the monogram results in *IAXO*, that is *Iacho*, which may be interpreted as Jacob or Jacobus. Read pin-wheel fashion, the chrismon gives *Rosa X* and may be decoded as Rosa Crux, or Rosae Cruxis, the rose cross.

Archaeological evaluation of the San Juan de la Peña Grail cup

In 1960, Professor Antonio Beltran, Chair of the Department of Archaeology at the University of Saragossa, was permitted to examine the cup in detail. He stated that—excluding the attached gold and ornaments (which date from the twelfth and fourteenth centuries)—the cup, measuring ca. 7 cm (2¾ in) in height and 9.5 cm (3¾ in) in diameter, could indeed be the Grail. It consists of a finely polished hollow agate. Its only ornament is a narrow groove that runs almost completely round the rim. It is Beltran's opinion that the cup originates from a Syrian or Palestinian workshop of the first century. The professor suggests

The above inscription can be read on the base of the cup under certain lighting conditions. The meaning of this mysterious inscription continues to puzzle experts. It has been deciphered as *lilzahira* ("for whom it blooms or glows").

Antioch, originally an extremely wealthy royal city, as the workshop's location. Since a stone cup would have been far too precious for a private home, only three possible patrons remain: the temple, the king, or a religious community.

The enigmatic inscription

In his *Parzival*, Wolfram von Eschenbach mentioned a mysterious inscription that appeared on the Grail. There is an Old Arabic (or Cufic) inscription on the foot of the San Juan de la Peña Grail, which was later attached to the older bowl. Professor Beltran interpreted the inscription as *il izahirati*, which can mean something like "for whom it blooms, or glows." Does the word "it" refer to God, or to Jesus, or to the Grail itself? Hans-Wilhelm Shäfer, a professor of Arabic, read the text completely differently, as *alabsit sillis*. This reading closely approximates Wolfram's Grail inscription, which spelled out *lapsit exillis* ("stone of the stars"). This may indicate that the Grail was brought to earth by angels. The *Parzival* Grail and that of the Pyrenéan monastery are remarkably similar in this respect.

Old Carcassonne is surrounded by powerful walls and was once a starting point for the campaigns against Cathars in the French Languedoc. Even today, its narrow lanes and intact ramparts impress numerous visitors.

THE FRENCH TRAIL

The Cathars and the Grail

The history of the Cathars, and especially their fall, is strongly connected with a particular mountain, which is Montségur in southern France. Like an eagle's nest, the impregnable Cathar fortress perched on the narrow crest of a mountain in the foothills of the Pyrenées. These days, the ruined walls of its successor are blasted by winds while the battlements leave visitors staggering at the sight of the deep ravines on every side of the site, gaping at the viewer like so many

mouths of hell. This rocky perch, it seems, could never have been conquered through force of arms. On all sides, a sheer drop of 200 to 260 feet (60–80 meters) of vertical rock face offers protection as effective as any fortress wall. The original Cathar castle was besieged by the troops of the French king for an entire year during the thirteenth century. Then, on March 16, 1244, the inhabitants of Montségur left their refuge— but not in surrender. Still refusing to renounce their faith, some 205 Cathars threw themselves, singing, onto a funeral pyre.

A tantalizing mystery

On the eve of March 16th, the Cathar leader Pierre-Rogère de Mirepoix was able to help four of his men escape by letting them down the western face of the mountain on ropes. Who were these four men, and why were they permitted to flee? Did they know important secrets, or were they conveying crucial documents or possessions (such as the Cathar treasure, for example) to safety? Their escape has given rise to a variety of speculations about this unusual secret sect. Is it possible that the Holy Grail was in the hands of these Cathars of Montségur, who furtively spirited it away from the king's troops that night?

After the long siege of Montségur by the king's troops (they could never have taken it by force), the exhausted inhabitants emerged voluntarily. The previous night, four Cathars had escaped by rope with an unidentified treasure.

The Cathar religion

The Christian Cathar sect developed in western Europe during the twelfth century. For the Cathars, the devil created all things visible and temporal, among which were the human body and sexuality. However, God created all things invisible and eternal, including the imperishable human soul. Thus pure people were bodiless, heavenly. The Cathar movement began quietly. Then a first Cathar diocese was established in the French Champagne; another developed in the region of Albi in southern France—hence the Cathars' other name, Albigensians. The Christian sect spread rapidly. Their heresy consisted mainly in the fact that they in a dualistic Christ. One was the earthly Christ who was crucified in Jerusalem (and rightly so, as he lived in sin with Mary Magdalene and even had children with her). The other was the heavenly Christ, who did not eat or drink, and was born and crucified in the invisible world.

Christ is only an angel

For the Cathars, Christ was an important prophet and teacher, but not the Savior, because he was merely an angel. Some radical Cathars believed that Christ had no physical body like everyone else, but only a *corpus phantasticum* (an illusory body). Every fallen soul is Christ's equal, believed the Cathars (whose name

means "pure ones"). But the Cathars valued their *parfaits* or *perfecti*, both of which mean "completed ones," even more highly than Christ.

The Cathars recognized Pope Innocent III as their most dangerous enemy. The pope sought to achieve the physical destruction of Catharism with the aid of imperial laws.

Alert explorers of the villages in former Cathar regions will discover ancient Cathar graves such as these at Saint-Engrâce, southeast of Biarritz. A simple grey stone with cross pattée marks the graves of the pure ones.

The mysterious sun room at Montségur

At the time these events took place, Montségur was the center of the Cathar movement. The French king's troops besieged the almost impregnable fortress on the rocky peak for an entire year. At last, the Cathars acceded to the ultimatum: it was agreed that the delivery of Montségur into the king's hands would take place on March 16, 1244.

Historians may have discovered why the heretics settled on this particular date to hand over control of their castle. In the year 1244, the equinox fell on March 15th. In Montségur, a sun room was oriented to the equinox was discovered. Did the Cathars delay their capitulation just enough to be able to hold some ritual celebration of the sun one last time? The mystery remains unresolved because everything that is known about the Cathars indicates that they not only rejected the practice of magic, but also (and especially) rituals.

A clue to the Grail?

The mysterious sun room in Montségur cannot be explained away. But what function might it have served? In light of Cathar theology, such a room could only have served as a place of transformation. A place in which, according to Cathar belief, people imprisoned in matter awoke and received the first beneficial rays of sunlight. Could it be that the Cathars were in possession of a cup that they used to carry out the sun ritual? Perhaps a cup made of gold or stones that caught the light? The Grail may be seen as a cauldron of renewal. The sun is the guarantor of all life on Earth. So, does the unusual existence of a sun room indicate the presence of the Grail, which was secreted away shortly before the destruction of the Cathars? We do not know with certainty, but many investigators think so.

The famous sun room of Montségur is located in this tower. Research shows that the sun's entrance into each sign of the zodiac corresponds with certain parts of the upper windows.

Each year on May 24th, the Roma and Sinti celebrate the arrival of the three Maries (Mary Magdalen, Mary Jacobe, and Mary Salome) in Saintes-Maries-de-la-Mer in the Camargue. Sarah, who is believed to have been Egyptian, may have been the Magdalen's maid.

Another Grail interpretation theory

The Cathars were certainly familiar with the idea that Christ had children with Mary Magdalen. This idea leads some researchers, such as the French author Jean Markale, to interpret the word *graal* in a whole new way. In fifteenth-century France, the Holy Grail, or *Saint Grail*, was called *sangréal* which is reminiscent of the French *sang royal* (royal blood). Is the Holy Grail, then, no less than a reference to a royal lineage founded by Jesus and Mary Magdalen? According to legend, Mary Magdalen arrived with her children in Razès, in the southern French Limousin (the later Cathar area), after she had been to Saintes-Marie-de-la-Mer on the shore of the Camargue, as the Roma and Sinti believe. Her children then founded a lineage from which the Merovingians later emerged.

The Grail as a document rather than a vessel

Interpreted in this light, the Cathar treasure would thus have been the proof of the existence of an authentic divine dynasty that had been thoroughly repressed by the Carolingian usurpers and their successors, the Capetians. Strangely enough, such a hypothesis corresponds with the Western European myth of a great monarch of divine lineage, a legendary world leader who would appear around the year 2000 CE. Thus some investigators, such as Jean Markale or the author team Michael Baigent and Richard Leigh, assert that it was not a cup that was removed just before the delivery of Montségur castle, but secret documents. These could not be allowed to fall into the hands of the French king or the pope because they proved that Jesus had descendants.

The famous Veil of Veronica does not get its name from a woman. By a wordplay, *vera icona* (true image) became Veronica. Almost certainly this was the cloth now at Manoppello.

THE ITALIAN TRAIL

Images from the Grail cycle in Italy

As mentioned earlier, an anonymous twelfth-century sculptor known to art historians as the Arthur Master represented parts of the Arthur cycle in the archivolt of the north portal of Modena cathedral. The portal is known as the *Porta della Peschiera* ("the Fishpond Portal"). Several scenes from the Arthur legend can be recognized, notably the rescue of Guinevere from the castle of Caradoc the giant. The Modena archivolt dates from between 1110 and 1130 and is thus the earliest known representation of Arthur in figurative art.

From 1165 comes Master Pantaleone's famous floor mosaic in Otranto cathedral. King Arthur (labelled *Arturus Rex*) can be found here, too, alongside Alexander the Great and the Greek gods (Arthur rides a symbolic goatlike animal). Finally, there is the representation of the Fisher King by an unknown sculptor at the little Romanesque village church in Mensano, near Siena (see p. 59).

The shroud of Christ

It is well known that the shroud of Christ is kept at Turin. On it is an image of the crucified one as well as various blood stains that resulted from that cruel execution. If the Shroud of Turin is venerated as an authentic relic, it must therefore "contain" the blood of the Savior. Various Grail narratives associate the Grail with this image of the crucified one. The idea is found in the Vulgate Cycle. for example (1215–1235; see pp. 38ff.). In this narrative, the crucified Jesus ascends from the Grail chalice. The same story is told in *Perlesvaus* (see box, p. 40), which even refers directly to the shroud of Jesus. In this story, Perlesvaus' sister wanted to acquire a piece of the shroud to secure the family's prosperity. At the end of the story, her fragment of the shroud was kept in the Grail chapel itself. Thus it is quite likely that some people venerated the shroud as the Holy Grail during the Middle Ages.

The Grail of Genoa
The Grail may also be found in vessel-form in Italy. In 1101, King Baldwin I (1058–1118) and his Frankish troops conquered Caesarea Maritima in Palestine with the aid of the Genoese fleet. The ancient Roman city became the seat of an archbishop and was settled not only by Franks, but also by Eastern Orthodox Christians and Muslims. As their share of the booty, the Genoans received a strange hexagonal bowl cut from a single emerald, the *sacro catino*, which they believed to be Jesus' cup of the Last Supper. The bowl was later brought back to Genoa and is currently kept in the church of San Lorenzo (or, rather, in the cathedral treasury)— although, unfortunately, the emerald turned out to be green glass. Other *sacri catino* exist in Italy, which are similarly seen as the authentic Holy Grail by their respective finders. One example is the cup sought out by the Grail scholar Gabriella Agrati.

The Volto Santo of Manoppello
A second relic, no less precious, is similarly venerated in Italy. This is the *volto santo* (or Veil of Veronica). Veronica's veil derives from the words *vera icona*, meaning the "true image" (of Jesus), a portrait which early Christians reported repeatedly, and has nothing to do with any woman named Veronica. One such representation, on a diaphanous veil, is the *volto santo* of Manoppello near Pescara in southern Italy. The most puzzling feature of the image on the veil is that it is neither painted nor woven (this has been confirmed microscopically). The face on this veil corresponds well with the portrait on the shroud of Turin. For the faithful, who venerate the veil as an image of the Savior himself, this is indeed the Holy Grail.

The Shroud of Turin shows the front and back of a man. Depending on the way it is laid out, viewers may have the impression that it has a doubled head, or two faces.

THE ENGLISH TRAIL

The mystery of Glastonbury

Glastonbury Abbey is believed to be the oldest Christian foundation in Britain. Its history begins in the eighth century CE, and it was only when the Glastonbury monks claimed to have made a significant discovery that it became connected with King Arthur. In 1191, these pious monks announced that they had excavated the abbey grounds and discovered the skeletons of the legendary King of Britain and his wife. They apparently also found an inscription which read, *Here lies the famous King Arturius, buried in the Isle of Avalon*. Avalon refers to the Celtic paradise, Otherworld, i. e., the next world. Neither the bones nor the wood bearing the inscription survive today. In 1962, the skilled archaeologist Dr. Ralegh Radford conducted further excavations on the spot indicated by the monks. He did indeed find an ancient grave, but there was no conclusive proof that it had once contained the mortal remains of King Arthur and Queen Guinevere. As a result of this alleged discovery, a steady stream of pilgrims found their way to Glastonbury, and the abbey became very wealthy.

Glastonbury and the Holy Grail

There is no conclusive proof that Joseph of Arimathea brought the Holy Grail to Glastonbury, as related by Robert de Boron (see pp. 30–33). Rather, research has tended to suggest that the abbey published a revised account of its own history in 1247. William of Malmesbury's first Glastonbury text of 1130, *De Antiquitate Glastoniensis Ecclesiae* (On the History of Glastonbury Abbey) does not include mention of

The red color of the water in Glastonbury's Chalice Well indicates the presence of iron. Immediately above this spring is a whitethorn shrub (in the background), a cutting from the original thorn, which still grows where it was planted (as legend has it) by Joseph of Arimathea.

Joseph of Arimathea. The later account, however, which was recorded in 1247, states that Joseph was the founder of the abbey. The original version stated merely that Glastonbury Abbey was founded by followers of Jesus. This might be seen as a deliberate fabrication of history.

The holy thorn of Glastonbury

Glastonbury's famous whitethorn is known for a botanical feature that has fascinated people throughout the centuries. According to the story, on his arrival from the Holy Land, Joseph of Arimathea staked his pilgrim staff into the ground. It took root and produced the original holy thorn, which flowers twice a year: once in the spring and once at Christmas. Botanists confirm that this whitethorn shrub originates from the Near East (hence the twice yearly flowering), and certify its great age. Every year, an Anglican priest cuts off a single branch and sends it to the Queen of England so that she can decorate her Christmas gift table with it.

The old abbey ruins at Glastonbury attract countless visitors, year after year. Many come to this atmospheric spot hoping to sense the spirit of King Arthur, whose grave is said to have been discovered here.

Strata Florida Abbey

One particular event links Glastonbury with the Cistercian monastery of Strata Florida in Wales (of which only a few ruins remain). This monastery claimed that after the dissolution of Glastonbury Abbey by order of King Henry VIII in 1539, seven of the ousted monks took refuge here. They brought with them their most precious relic, an olive wood bowl or cup, which was blackened with age. It was Glastonbury Abbey's original Communion chalice, which would have been used every Sunday to celebrate the Mass. But this olive wood cup, which apparently had the power to heal the sick, could only be the Holy Grail (that is, Jesus' chalice of the Last Supper). The cup later came into the possession of the wealthy, aristocratic Powell family from Nanteos, and became widely known as the Nanteos Cup. It remained in the Powell family until the last of them died in the 1950s, and its current whereabouts are not firmly established.

The intersecting circles on the gate to the Chalice Well Garden symbolize the merging of the terrestrial and celestial worlds. Does the Holy Grail lie at the interface?

New Grail discoveries in Glastonbury

There is an ancient legend which says that Joseph of Arimathea buried Christ's cup of the Last Supper near the foot of Glastonbury Tor. Ever since then, that spot has gushed water into a stone basin from a healing spring known as the Chalice Spring. The iron-rich water is reddish brown and is believed to have helped many people. It feeds a well, known as the Chalice Well, which was built in approximately 1184 of solid stone and consists of two chambers. In about 1958, the Chalice Well Trust created an idyllic garden around the ancient spring. Innumerable pilgrims visit the Chalice Well annually to drink its pure spring water. Beliefs that the spring may once have been a Druidic cult site cannot be supported. Excavations have shown that the whole area was settled no earlier than the Roman period, ca. 200 BCE. But the Chalice Spring, and the Chalice Well, have survived and continued to be of enormous interest for hundreds of years because of another discovery connected with its environs.

King Arthur's Round Table

Believed genuine, this is the famous round table at which King Arthur gathered the best knights in the land, the same table at which the knights were served by the Grail. It may be seen in the Great Hall of Winchester Castle (built in 1067) in southern England. The great circular table, with its twenty-four alternating green and white segments, hangs on a wall in the otherwise empty room, and can accommodate (as may be inferred from the names around the perimeter) twenty-four knights. Enthroned at the top is King Arthur, and the names of the rest of his company can be read clockwise: Sir Galahallt, Sir Launcelot, Sir Gauen, Sir Percyvale, Sir Lyonell, Sir Trystam, Sir Garethe, Sir Bedwere, Sir Blubrys, Sir Lacotemale, Sir Lucane, Sir Plomyd, Sir Lamorak, Sir Born, Sir Safer, Sir Pelleus, Sir Kay, Sir Ectorde, Sir Dagonet, Sir Degore, Sir Brumear, Sir Lybyus, Sir Alynore, and Sir Mordrede. This is therefore a complete list of the Knights of the Round Table, even though the table itself—which still holds many people under its spell—has been dendrochronologically dated to the thirteenth century.

The Grail in Hertford

The ongoing lure of the Grail was demonstrated in May 2005 when two latter-day Templars, building on the success of *The Da Vinci Code*, drew attention to a labyrinth of tunnels under the ancient town of Hertford, north of London. The tunnels connect with Hertford Castle, where in 1309 four Knights Templar were imprisoned by King Edward II, who believed they held a lost treasure. That lost treasure, rumored to include the Holy Grail, may still lie hidden in this underground maze. However, the tunnels could not be investigated as they had been bricked up, and (the Templars explained) were even booby-trapped in places. This did not prevent film crews from Australia, Germany, and Britain's Channel 4 from seeking to enter them. A segment made for Australia's *60 Minutes* program was broadcast internationally—and drew record ratings.

It is unlikely that the Knights of the Round Table ever sat at this table. But the circular table top impresses everyone who sees it in Winchester Castle with its great size and design.

The sapphire blue bowl

At the beginning of the twentieth century, an unusual bowl was discovered in a field close to the Chalice Well. The finder, an esotericist named Wellesley Tudor Pole (1884–1968), was no less mysterious than the sapphire blue bowl—which, he explained, was the true Grail. This took place in 1906, and the cup remained in a chapel in Bristol until 1914. According to reports, the bowl defied scientific dating for many years, and its place of manufacture could not be clarified either. It is still not permitted to film or photograph the Grail of the Chalice Well. However, some scholars were granted permission to examine it recently, and it turned out that the sapphire blue glass could have been made in Venice, ca. 1880.

THE GRAIL – AN ETERNAL MYSTERY

Even the first coherent literary history of the Holy Grail (by Chrétien de Troyes, 1180, see pp 20ff.) remained incomplete. Why the author failed to complete it, or to tell his audience more about the origin and appearance of the Grail, will probably never be understood. The Grail remains the greatest *mysterium* of the West. To all intents and purposes, it is rooted here in the Western world, even though some historical conceptual components clearly derive from the influences of Islam and the ancient Persian faith. Reading the various ancient and modern texts on the Grail, one can hardly avoid the impression that the Grail is a compelling myth with its origin in the human psyche.

Quite a few contemporary researchers interpret the Grail as a feminine symbol (in its capacity as a bowl capable of bearing), and the accompanying bleeding lance as the male phallus. The pure ambiguity and indeterminacy of the Grail—whether it is chalice, stone, dish, cauldron, or *volto santo*—prevents us from forming a clear understanding of its true nature. This allows it to be discovered, and discovered again, by future generations.

The Templars believed the Grail was the chalice used by Jesus at the Last Supper. Other researchers believe, on the contrary, that the military knights' quest for the Grail was to find the physical children of Jesus and Mary Magdalen.

The musical *Monty Python's Spamalot* is based on the film *Monty Python and the Holy Grail*. It treats the idea of King Arthur and the Holy Grail—as well as the relationship between the French and the English—as a satirical "Grail Comedy."

An image of the eternal divine

The Grail quest is notable for the extraordinary passion of those who undertake it, as well as the tribulations and dangers the seeker must endure. Those wishing to achieve the Grail must undergo profound inner transformation. Thus it is clear that people see the Grail as a symbol of the eternal divine within human beings, which yearns for humanity (as the mystics express it) as humanity yearns for it. By its very nature, then, the Grail must be achieved over and over again— a never-ending quest to which individual seekers may devote their entire lifetimes. As long as this occurs, the Grail will remain alive, revealing further, hitherto unknown aspects of itself as time goes by.

Although people always seek to approach the Grail, it can never be pinned down. Thus it lives on in the realm of human imagination. What cannot be clearly identified becomes a fount of speculation and mythology.

GRAIL TIMELINE

30	A cup or chalice was used at Jesus' Last Supper with the apostles in Jerusalem
62	Peter brings the Grail—the Last Supper chalice—to Rome
67	Supposed execution of Peter in Rome
70	Destruction of Jerusalem by the Romans
258	Cup of the Last Supper (Grail cup) sent to Huesca, Spain

Max Bruckner employed both imagination and a mastery of perspective when he created the stage sets for Richard Wagner's *Parsifal*. His coulisses in Bayreuth still convey a contemporary spirit of the age.

485–488	Arthur fights against the Angles
493	Arthur triumphs in the Battle of Badon over the Angles and Saxons
519	Death of King Arthur at the Battle of Camlann
717	Earliest reference to the Grail, by the Breton hermit Helinandus
924	Foundation of San Juan de la Peña monastery
1099	The Crusaders conquer Jerusalem
1076	The Grail cup comes to San Juan de la Peña
1100	King Arthur named as King of the Britons in the *Chronicle of Mont-Saint-Michel*
1110/30	The Modena archivolt (north portal of cathedral) decorated with an Arthurian scene
1119	Knights Templar established in Jerusalem
1123/50	Creation of the "Grail-Bearer" fresco at San Climente, Tahull
1139	Geoffrey of Monmouth completes *Historia Regum Britanniae*, putting the King Arthur tradition into writing for the first time
1150	Dietrich of Flanders brings the blood of Jesus to Bruges
1159	The seal of a Portuguese title deed to the Templars refers to the Grail with the words *Por tuo Gral*
1165	King Arthur is shown in the floor mosaic of Otranto cathedral
ca. 1180	Chrétien de Troyes writes *Perceval*
1190	Glastonbury monks unearth the bones of Arthur and Guinevere

Edwin Austin Abbey's sumptuous painting *Galahad at the Castle of the Grail* (1895) underscores yet again how powerfully the very idea of the Grail stimulates the artistic imagination.

Mary Magdalen and the Grail depicted together in a church window. Does the artist invite the viewer to choose between the chalice or the Magdalen as the vehicle of God?

Further Reading

Baigent, Michael, Leigh, Richard, and Lincoln, Henry. *Holy Blood, Holy Grail*. New York: Dell Publishing, 1983

Bennett, Janice. *St. Laurence and the Holy Grail: The Story of the Holy Chalice of Valencia*. Fort Collins: Ignatius Press, 2002

Cotterell, Maurice. *Jesus, King Arthur, and the Journey of the Grail: The Secrets of the Sun Kings*. Rochester, NY: Bear and Company, 2006

Martin, Sean. *The Knights Templar: The History and Myths of the Legendary Order*. New York: Thunders' Mouth Press, 2004

McKitterick, Rosamond, ed. *Atlas of the Medieval World*. New York: Oxford University Press, 2004

O'Shea, Stephen. *The Perfect Heresy: The Revolutionary Life and Spectacular Death of the Medieval Cathars*. New York: Walker and Company, 2001

Pagels, Elaine. *The Gnostic Gospels: A Startling Account of the Meaning of Jesus and the Origin of Christianity Based on Gnostic Gospels and Other Secret Texts*. New York: Random House, 2004

Rahn, Otto. *Crusade Against the Grail: The Struggle between the Cathars, the Templars, and the Church of Rome*. Rochester, NY: Inner Traditions, 2006 (first published 1933)

Starbird, Margaret. *The Tarot Trumps and The Holy Grail*. Boulder, CO: Woven Word Press, 2000

Picture Credits

INDEX